ADHD and ME:
Beyond the mask

Kayleigh Osben

Contents

About the Author

Dedication

Prologue

Chapter One - Unseen threads

Poems – *"A late diagnosis of ADHD", "Defying the stats"*

Chapter Two – Childhood

Poems – *"The bottom of Mum's Garden", "Sensitive", "Masking", "I Cry for Her"*

Chapter Three – Finding my way (and losing it too)

Poem – *"I fell"*

Chapter Four – Breaking the Chains

Poems - *"Narcissist", "It's a feeling that is a little hard to explain"*

Chapter Five – Neurodivergence in our Family

Poems – *"ADD they call it", "I lose things",*

Chapter Six – The ADHD Traits in me

Poems – *"Wouldn't it be nice?", "Out of Sight", "Too Much", "Worth", "Impostor", "Burnout", "Social Anxiety", "Attention Deficit"*

Chapter Seven – The Lost Week- PMDD

Chapter Eight – Work that Moves Me

Chapter Nine – Navigating the System

Poems – *"Fighting for something that doesn't exist", "Assumptions", "School Mornings", "Party", "Neurodivergence awareness week", "Child's Mental Health"*

Chapter Ten – Born to Mother

Poems – *"Hold on to each stage", "Single Mum", "School Mornings", "Five minutes peace", "One Day"*

Chapter Eleven – The weight of it all

Poem – *"I've been to the bottom", "Rest if you must"*

Chapter Twelve: How Tinder became my emotional growth app

Poem – *"Tinder"*

Chapter Thirteen – Negative Relationships

Poems – *"My Soul", "They spent the night together", "Fraud", "Are you thinking about me too", " Twin Flames", "Unspoken", "Weighted Blanket", "I guess that's not me", "She's lost and she's not being found", "The nice guy disguise", "They fought, I was weak", "The Shadow of who she was", "The things I want to say", "I fell for you", "She knows"*

Chapter Fourteen – Rising again

Poem – *"Therapy taught me", "Seeds of Intention", "Wouldn't it be boring"*

ADHD Self-Help Toolkit

1) Reframing Failures: From Shame to Growth

2) **Late Diagnosis ADHD Checklist**

3) **Rejection Sensitivity Checklist**

4) **Affirmations for Healing and Empowerment**

5) **Life with ADHD – Practical Hacks**

6) **Spirituality and Intention Setting**

7) **Letting Go and Moving Forward**

8) **ADHD Mothers toolkit**

List of useful resources

Final Message from *beyond the mask*

Authors Note

References

About the Author

Kayleigh Osben is a writer, mother, SEND professional, and late-diagnosed neurodivergent woman who has spent her life turning pain into purpose. A graduate with a first-class degree and a BPS-accredited master's in psychology, Kayleigh's journey has been shaped not only by her academic achievements but by her lived experiences navigating life as a single parent to five neurodivergent children.

Diagnosed with ADHD later in life, Kayleigh brings a deeply personal and insightful lens to neurodivergence, mental health, and the resilience of the human spirit. Her passion for inclusive education, her work within SEND services, and her drive to empower other women have made her a trusted voice in the world of advocacy and lived-experience leadership.

ADHD and ME: Beyond the Mask is more than a memoir - it's a testimony of survival, healing, and radical self-acceptance. Through poetry, reflection, and raw honesty, Kayleigh invites readers to honour their truth, embrace their difference, and find power in their voice.

She lives in Essex, UK, with her children, where she continues to write, advocate, and support others on their journeys through neurodiversity, trauma recovery, and self-discovery.

Dedication

For my children
You have taught me more than any degree ever could.
You are the reason I grow.
You are the reason I am me.

"Her story isn't mine, but the way she tells it gripped me. I was in awe of the emotion and truth in every line" – SEND Education and Mental Health Professional – early reader

"Kayleigh Osben opens a door into her world of ADHD with this brave and honest collection of memoir and poetry. Pass through that doorway, let her walk you through her many experiences from childhood to the present, evoking sadness, joy and hope, whatever your gender, personal label, diagnosis or not, you will identify with so much within these pages. The relatable shared accounts of happenings, responses and reactions leave one with a feeling of not being alone – Anna Mae author of: A Bit of Spirit and a lot of Spit

With Thanks

I want to express my sincere gratitude to author and poet Anna Mae for the inspiration and motivation she provided me to begin writing my book. Her courage to share honestly and her ability to turn personal truth into powerful words gave me the permission I needed to start telling my own story.

Thank you also to BoHo Banter in Clacton, the first place where I publicly shared my poetry. The warmth and encouragement I received from this community helped me build the confidence to believe in my voice and continue writing. That space became the foundation of this journey.

With heartfelt thanks,

Kayleigh Osben

Prologue

This is not just a book of poems. It is a collection of pieces of me, fragments of a life shaped by trauma, love, loss, resilience, and the winding path of discovering who I truly am. It's the story of growing up feeling different, of trying to fit into a world that didn't seem built for me, of masking, of breaking, and of slowly, painfully, learning to rise.

For most of my life, I didn't have the words for why I felt the way I did. I just knew I was always on the outside looking in, watching, copying, trying to blend in. I didn't know that I was neurodivergent. I didn't know that my brain worked differently, that my struggles weren't failures, but signs of a mind wired in its own unique, powerful way.

This book traces that journey. From childhood to parenthood, through toxic relationships and healing, through moments of despair and sparks of hope. It's about what it means to fall down, to lose yourself, and to find a way back - again and again.

If you've ever felt different, unworthy, or unseen, I hope these words remind you that you are not alone. That difference is not something to hide, but something to honour. That our scars don't make us weak - they are the places where our strength shines through.

These pages hold my truth. I offer them to you, with the hope that they might help you find your own.

Chapter 1
Unseen Threads

My brother, sister and I grew up with holes in our shoes and hunger tucked between our ribs, children of poverty, trying to stitch ourselves into a world that never quite felt made for us. The hand-me-downs, the broken kitchen cupboards, the quiet shame of free school meals - they shaped us but never defined us.

Back then, I thought the world was hard because life was hard. I didn't have the words for why I felt out of step, why making friends seemed like trying to catch the wind. I learned to mask, to mimic, to survive - never knowing that the reason I struggled wasn't just the weight of poverty, but the invisible threads of neurodivergence woven through my mind.

I was unaware, too, that our mother walked the same path in silence, living with undiagnosed autism and ADHD, fighting her own invisible battles while raising us the best she could. Her struggles were hidden in plain sight, like ours, mistaken for other things: stress, sensitivities, hardship.

It wasn't until my own children began their journeys - diagnosed, supported, named- that I started to look inward. To see in myself, and in my mother, what we had long overlooked. At 36, I was diagnosed with ADHD, and so much of my past came into focus. The chaos, the passion, the overwhelm, the quiet battles no one saw, all finally had a name.

And yet, despite it all, the poverty, the confusion, the feeling of not quite belonging, my brother, my sister, and I defied the odds. We each found our way through education's maze. We graduated. We became postgraduates. We rose from disadvantage and made something of the very traits that once made us feel out of place.

Living with ADHD has meant I've often struggled with relationships, finding myself drawn into unhealthy patterns, caught in controlling or abusive dynamics, searching for safety where I rarely found it. That, too, is part of my story, and some of these poems give voice to that pain and the journey to heal.

But what ADHD has also given me is fire: the fierce, unstoppable drive to advocate for my children. To fight for their rights, their education, their safety. Some of the poems in this book reflect that part of me - the mother, the warrior, the voice that refuses to be silenced.

This book is for the younger versions of me. For my siblings. For our mother. For anyone who grew up thinking they were simply wrong, when really, they were simply different and deserved to be understood.

The poems woven within this book are pieces of that journey.

A late diagnosis of ADHD

A late diagnosis of ADHD,
Came with relief and sadness for me,
All of them years doubting my brain,
Wondering why I didn't think quite the same,
Often an outsider in primary school,
I'd long to fit in, but I didn't at all,
That's when I learned a skill I would master,
I became A star type of masker,
My school reports state, 'She needs to try harder,
Maths and spelling are skills she just doesn't harbour.'
But you see, it wasn't a lack of skill,
It's just boring work, and I couldn't sit still,
Give me a topic of my desire,
And I'll learn all about and be a high flyer,
Intellectually bright and I can solve any puzzle,
Creative, artistic, I work well in a muddle,
I can thrive in chaos and work well under pressure,
The love and passion I have are something to treasure,
And so, it's important and it's not just a label,
Young people should know what they bring to the table.

Defying the stats

My brother, sister and I, we defied the stats,
Because when we were born into poverty, we weren't destined for graduation hats,
We started life in Langham Drive, a flat in Clacton-on-Sea,
And we lived our early years surrounded by poverty,
Where mould draped the walls and noise polluted the air,
And statistically, there was no hope for us there,
We moved into a house when I was about three,
And there we had a garden, my brother, sister and me,
But poverty followed us when my dad left our Mum,
And statistically in our lives, university wouldn't be done,
But we defied the odds, we shone brighter than predicted,
And we all graduated and went against the statistic,
Not just one graduation, we are post-grads too,
And there is no limit to anything we can do,
My sister a Dr has gained her PhD,
And I've got a master's in psychology,
My brother a nurse consultant with an MPAC,
You wouldn't have thought we'd come this far if you had looked back,
And so don't let your roots determine what you can be,
You can defy the odds like my brother, sister and me.

Chapter Two
Childhood

Our childhood wasn't clean or simple; it was messy, tangled with moments of joy and pain, woven with both freedom and fear. There was laughter in our beautiful garden, where we were like 'free-range' children. We weren't bound by strict rules, and other kids loved coming to spend time with us, camping in the garden, sharing campfires, tasting a kind of wild freedom.

But my early years weren't so free. The first four years of my life were shadowed by domestic violence. My father, perhaps neurodivergent himself and struggling with undiagnosed challenges, turned to alcohol and drugs. I witnessed his anger tear holes not just through the doors of our home, but through the fragile safety of my childhood. I remember the fights, they would get so bad that we'd have to run, my brother, sister and I, fleeing to my nan and grandad's house just a few doors away. I can still picture us bolting out the front door, barefoot and crying, our small legs carrying us as fast as we could to safety.

There were times hiding beneath the bed with my mother and siblings, trembling at raised voices, the sound of fists on walls, dreading his return. That kind of fear burns into you. It becomes part of your nervous system. Your baseline.

And yet, my father wasn't only a man of rage. He could be tender too, a man of contradictions, like a real-life Jekyll and Hyde. He called me his princess, hugged me, and soothed me to sleep. I remember that softness as well. But at age four, a memory carved itself into my heart: he sat me on his knee, told me I was his princess, and that he was leaving. That moment haunted my dreams for years, even as his leaving brought a strange kind of relief. Without him, we lived more freely, away from the grip of violence.

But that early experience shaped me deeply. It shaped how I would come to see men, how I would understand love, how I would question my worth and struggle with self-esteem. I saw other adults, especially men, fight to be part of their children's lives. I watched my mother's new partner battle to gain access to his daughter, going through courts, writing letters, never giving up. And yet, my own father never fought for me. I have one memory etched sharply: I was dressed up, my siblings and I waiting outside our house in our best clothes, excited to see our dad. But he never came. The excuse? Hay fever. But even at that young age, I knew it was something else. Addiction. Shame.

Avoidance. Whatever the reason, he chose not to show up. And that wounded me in a way no one could see.

No man fought for me. Not him. Not the other men who entered my life through my mother's relationships. And many of those men only added to the damage. Reinforcing the belief that men could not be trusted. That I was not protected. That I didn't matter.

These early relationships taught me to expect pain, to accept abandonment, to confuse control with love. They planted seeds of mistrust and shame; seeds I would spend decades untangling.

And yet, even among all of this, the chaos, the violence, the neglect, there were moments of beauty. The garden. The open sky. The imagination that bloomed in wild spaces. I still go to the bottom of that garden sometimes when I need calm, when the world feels too much. It reminds me of the duality of my childhood, how pain and freedom often lived side by side.

Dad

My heart was first broken at the age of four,
I remember it well when my dad left the door,
He sat me on his lap at the end of the bed,
He told me I was his princess and kissed me on my head,
But he left and was gone, hardly saw him again,
Then he passed away when I had just turned ten,
I didn't know how to feel at the time,
But he was the only man I could have ever called mine,
So, as I get older, I realise what I've missed,
The importance of that cuddle and his last ever kiss.

As I mentioned above, our childhood, although tainted with trauma, wasn't all bad; in fact, there were moments of pure joy. While our childhood was tangled with difficulty, it wasn't without beauty. Our mother, though struggling herself with undiagnosed neurodivergence, tried her best to create magic out of the ordinary. She gave what she could with what little she had, and in doing so, left us with memories that still warm the heart.

I remember teddy bears' picnics in the garden, where we'd lie out blankets, bring our toys to life, and pretend the world was nothing but kind. I remember long walks through our beautiful village, where the wind would catch our laughter and carry it down country lanes. These were simple moments, yet they stitched joy into the fabric of our childhood. Some of my most joyful childhood memories are rooted not in toys or technology but in the feeling of being outside, wild, free, and untamed. And I know I'm not alone in this.

Research shows that many of us hold our fondest early memories outdoors. If you pause for a moment and think about your own, I'd guess at least one of them takes place under an open sky - maybe on a hot summer day, when the air smelled of grass and possibility. Not for everyone, of course, but for many of us, nature was our first playground and our truest sense of freedom.

Time spent outdoors has so many benefits and has even been linked with lower rates of anxiety and depression in later life (McCurdy et al., 2010). Studies have shown that the outdoors can be a powerful ally for the ADHD brain. Natural environments offer the movement, sensory input, and freedom that many neurodivergent children need to thrive. In fact, when you watch a group of children playing freely outside, climbing, exploring, and creating, you often can't tell which ones have ADHD. It's only when they're all sitting in a classroom, expected to stay still, quiet, and focused on abstract tasks, that the differences become visible. The issue isn't that these children can't learn - it's that the environment doesn't always fit the way their brains are wired to learn best.

And yet, so much of childhood today is spent confined within four classroom walls - six hours a day, five days a week - during the most formative years of our lives. We're expected to sit still, suppress our instincts, and absorb knowledge through a rigid structure, often at the expense of play and exploration.

One of my most treasured memories is from a time we went to *Glastonbury Festival* - not as adults chasing music, but as children on a wild adventure. My mum took my brother, sister and me, and we camped right next to the woods. I remember how the forest felt like a living thing, welcoming us in. We played for hours, filthy with mud, climbing, running, laughing. I felt completely free - no expectations, no pressures, just a child in nature, being.

It stirred something deep in my soul - a feeling I still chase to this day when I walk barefoot in the grass or sit beneath the trees. That first trip to Glastonbury lit a spark in me. That trip has stayed etched in my memory not for what we saw or bought, but for how I *felt* - alive, connected, and completely free.

It's easy to focus on the painful memories - those that left marks, those we're still trying to make sense of. Trauma has a way of casting long shadows. But healing doesn't always come from reliving the pain. Sometimes, it comes from remembering the light.

That's why I've chosen to include these memories, because my childhood wasn't only made up of wounds. It was also made up of wonder.

I share these moments I treasure - the glimpses of joy, freedom, and comfort that gave me a sense of who I truly was before the world told me who I had to be. These memories remind me that there was always beauty, even in the mess.

As you read, I invite you to pause and reflect on your own moments of joy. They don't need to be big or dramatic. Sometimes the smallest memories carry the most warmth. Take a moment to think of one. Let it sit with you. You can even write it down in the reflection pages at the back of this book - because your story matters, too.

One of the magic moments of my childhood was Christmas time. We didn't have much, money was tight, and luxuries were rare, but somehow, Mum made sure the magic of Christmas never faded. She kept the spirit alive in ways that didn't cost much but meant everything. It wasn't about big presents or flashy decorations; it was about the feeling, the traditions, the love stitched into every detail.

Our stockings weren't the fancy kind you see in shops today. They were made from tight material, the type you wear, placed gently at the foot of our beds. Inside were little gifts, simple things, but each chosen with care. And always, always a tangerine nestled at the toe. That was tradition.

Each year, one of us would receive the "main" present, something slightly bigger or extra special, while the others had stockings filled with thoughtful bits and pieces.

We never complained. We understood the rotation, and it felt fair. We were happy. Truly happy. We appreciated the little things, the togetherness, the way Mum always made it feel magical even when she had so little to give.

What stays with me now isn't the gifts themselves, but the memory of waking up on Christmas morning, the soft rustle of wrapping paper, the excitement in the air. The feeling of being loved. That's the magic she gave us, one we carry still.

Despite the chaos and the lack of a strong support network, love was always there, raw and real. The weight of raising us fell solely on her shoulders, and though the burden was heavy, she carried it with grit and a fierce kind of love.

Our mum has always been a passionate and driven woman. Her strong sense of justice, her determination, and her deep belief in us shaped who we are. She planted the belief early that we could do anything we set our minds to - a lesson that echoed through everything I later achieved.

The moments I cherish most were the ones when it was just us, my mum, my brother, my sister, and me. In those moments, there was peace. There was safety. There was love

The Bottom of Mum's Garden

for the place where magic first found me

At the bottom of the garden, where the wild things grew,
Where nettles tangled secrets and old breezes blew,
We lit our first campfires and toasted marshmallows too,
Where smiles and laughter were plenty and worries were few,

The grass bent kindly beneath our bare feet,
As we played made-up games and had picnics to eat,
We built crooked dens from old sticks and wood,
And the energy was high; it always felt good.

This was our forest, our meadow, our land,
Where scraped knees and laughter went hand in hand.
We camped under skies that never felt far,
With the hum of the hedgerow and one steadfast star.

The green held our joy in its infinite seams,
Our breath stitched into soil, our roots and our dreams.
just the wild birds singing and the whisper of bees,
Surrounded by farmland and trees.

Even now, when the world feels heavy and wide,
I go to that field in the folds of my mind.
To the bottom of Mum's Garden, my first sacred ground,
Where the child I once was can still be found.

Christmas Magic

Early morning, the Christmas lights glow,
As sleepy children stir, *he's been, he's been!*
Stockings are filled, the mince pie and carrot gone,
The presents are waiting, the tree glistens green.

There are smiles and giggles, gasps of delight,
Wrapping paper scattered across the floor,
Laughter rings out as hearts feel light,
Toys unboxed, excitement galore.

The turkey in the oven, filling the air,
With the scent of comfort, joy, and cheer.
The table's laid with mismatched plates,
Extra chairs pulled in, family near.

It's messy, loud, imperfectly sweet,
But love and magic fill the space,
This is the moment, the memories we keep,
Not things, but warmth we can't replace.

Christmas magic lives in all these small things,
In laughter, love, and the chaos it brings.
So don't chase perfection, let joy be enough,
And have a Merry Christmas, wrapped in love.

I was a sensitive child, always emotional, always carrying this quiet, ongoing narrative in my mind that I was unlovable, different, somehow older than my years. The smallest things could upset me, and I felt things deeply, often more than I knew how to express. I didn't know why I felt so different. ADHD wasn't something I'd heard of back then. I just knew I didn't seem to experience the world the same way others did.

One thing that ran strong in me, and in my family, was a deep sense of justice. I felt passionate about what was right and wrong, even as a child. I see now that this is something many neurodivergent people share: that fierce, unshakeable drive for fairness. But at the time, I wasn't understood. Instead of being seen for what I was, a child with undiagnosed ADHD, I was labelled. *Attention seeker. Drama queen.* Words that stung, words that followed me, when really, what I needed was understanding.

When I got emotional or upset, my mum didn't always know how to respond. She herself was undiagnosed autistic at the time, and that meant she often struggled with emotional reciprocity, not because she didn't care, but because she didn't know the "right" things to say or do. I found it hard to process my emotions, and I began to feel bad for even feeling them. But looking back now, I want to challenge a common misconception: **it wasn't that my mother lacked empathy**, as so many mistakenly believe of autistic people.

In fact, autistic individuals often experience *deep and intense empathy*, sometimes even more so than neurotypical individuals. What they may struggle with is *cognitive empathy*, or the ability to understand another's emotional state in the moment and respond in socially expected ways, not the *emotional empathy* that underpins care, concern, and connection (Baron-Cohen & Wheelwright, 2004).

Autistic people often report experiencing **"empathic distress,"** where they feel another's pain so intensely that it becomes overwhelming (Bird et al., 2010). The difficulty is not a lack of empathy, but an overflow of it, paired with challenges in expressing it conventionally. My mum loved deeply, and she cared deeply. She just didn't always know how to show it in the ways the world expected her to.

Rejection sensitivity runs deep in people with ADHD; it feels like a physical pain. And I felt it hard, even as a child. Every perceived or real rejection cut deep. I was told I was too emotional, too sensitive. But now I know it was more than that. I remember the distress I felt when my mum was out at council meetings, advocating and standing up for what she believed in. I'd wait at the window for her to come home, longing for the safety of her presence.

In our home, neurodivergence was just part of life; our differences weren't questioned, they simply were. It was at school where I felt that difference most sharply. I knew I struggled socially and emotionally. I struggled to read and write in the ways they expected. My school report said I needed to try harder. That I was a daydreamer. Easily distracted. But in truth, my brain worked differently. It didn't mean I wasn't intelligent - far from it. I was, and am, highly intelligent. I just didn't learn the same way as everyone else.

Sensitive

She's just sensitive, that's what they say,
They don't see things in her way,
She's emotional and
They say she cries over silly things,
But the tears that roll down her cheeks
They sting,
It's a feeling that's felt deep to the core,
A feeling that makes her feel she can't breathe anymore,
You make a comment that makes her feel rejected,
And her reaction is a little unexpected,
She's just sensitive and overreacting,
Despite the effect that comment is having,
She turns her feelings into jokes,
You don't appreciate when they are spoke,
But if you knew how she's been treated before,
You'd understand why is not safe to say how she feels anymore,
The words that twist and wind inside,
Are flowing like an unruly tide,
She wants to run, to hide and be gone,
Fight, flight and freeze are coming through strong,
But she's just sensitive, or so they say,
Or could it be more than that today

I remember my self-esteem as a child being painfully low. I felt different, and I was treated differently. At primary school, I was often isolated, always on the edge of things, watching but not quite part of it all.

I did have a couple of friends. Outside of school, I'd play with them, running around the fields, climbing trees, riding bikes. But at school, it was different. They didn't want to be seen with me, not really. Not when it mattered. I was the girl most people avoided, the one who got picked on, and they didn't want that to rub off on them. So even the friends I thought I had kept their distance when the classroom walls surrounded us.

One memory has stayed with me. I must have been around 9. There was a boy in our class who had been on television, just an advert, but at that age, it made him feel like a star. All the girls crowded around him, asking for his autograph, holding out their arms like he was someone famous. I didn't care about the autograph, not really. But I saw what everyone else was doing, and I wanted to belong. So, I joined in, held out my arm only for him to look at me with disgust and push it away.

That rejection stung. It wasn't about the autograph. It was about wanting to be included, to be seen the same as everyone else. But I wasn't. I was different. My mum was raising us alone, and we weren't always well presented. But more than that, I didn't know how to be socially. I didn't know how to fit in. That was the moment I really started to learn how to mask, to try, to bend myself into shapes that might make me feel like I belonged. To hide the parts of me that felt too different.

Masking

Imagine living life but never having a break,
A full-time acting job,
trying not to seem fake,
Your brain is always active, planning the next script,
Trying to be part of a society you don't seem to fit,
Always pretending to be 'just fine',
But in reality, masking all the time,
Which character will be first, and what needs to be done?
Planning every possible social interaction,
Rehearsal and performance on repeat,
All the while trying to stay happy and upbeat,
But masking is exhausting, and it burns you out,
Leaves you with anxiety and self-doubt,
And so, we need a society that accepts everyone,
So that masking isn't something that needs to be done,
Imagine a world where we could all be ourselves,
And not have to pretend to be someone else,
Freely stimming, singing and being unique,
Not focused on a set persona and physique,
Colourful, creative, out of the box,
With free-flowing thoughts and wearing odd socks,
Let's dare to be different, be brave and be you,
And hopefully, others will feel safe to be themselves, too.

Around the age of ten, I faced more trauma - my first real experiences of grief and loss. The one that hit me hardest at the time is something I will not write about in detail here, but know that it was heartbreaking, tragic, and it crushed a part of me.

I didn't feel entitled to grieve. I was just a child, and I struggled to validate my own feelings. My self-esteem was so low that I didn't feel worthy of having big feelings. I felt like grief was something I had no right to - like even my sadness wasn't valid.

Not long before that, just two days before my tenth birthday, I lost my dad. He hadn't been a constant in our lives; we'd only seen him on and off since I was eight, but I still remember his last visit. He came to give us Christmas presents, told us how much he loved us. It was as if he knew somehow that it would be the last time. He died soon after - we were told it was his heart, though later I learned the truth: he had taken heroin and choked on his own vomit.

I remember my mum calling my friend's house, where I was staying at the time. I walked home and she sat me, my brother, and my sister down to tell us that Dad had died. Afterwards, I walked back to my friend's, and as I looked up, I saw rays of sunlight breaking through the clouds. *That's him,* I thought. *That's Dad, going up to heaven.* That memory stays with me, clear as day.

I didn't let myself feel the grief at the time. I went on with life as if it hadn't touched me. At his funeral, everything felt surreal, distant. I kept thinking: *Who am I to be sad about my dad?* A man who hadn't really been in my life since I was four. Was I even allowed to feel this pain? My self-esteem was so low, I didn't even feel worthy of mourning.

I cry for her, the little girl I once was,

And pain fills my veins because I know she was lost,
Craving comfort, attention, safety and love,
But always feeling not good enough,
That feeling was deepened by bullies at school,
They called her names and were oh so cruel,
She wasn't understood and was called a drama queen,
And when she showed her emotions, people were mean
She was rejected and cast aside by most of her peers,
And nightmares were had of her deepest fears,
She woke in the night, sobbing sometimes,
And called out for some love of any kind,
But darkness was there as the recurring theme,
As she relived her trauma in the shape of a dream,
But I'm not her anymore, stuck trembling with fear,
At the fights that were had fueled with alcohol and beer,
There aren't holes in the doors or dirt on the floor,
She's safe in a home she created and more,
She's looking up now, proud of who she's become,
A hardworking woman and loving Mum,
She's free from the past, and she's not scared anymore,
She's created an empire, she's the empress for sure,
And so I wrap my arms around that little girl who is me,
Carry her through the fire, and now together we are free.

Chapter Three:
Finding My Way (and Losing It Too)

My teenage years were better, in some ways. Life began to lift a little. My mum got a job, and for the first time, we weren't living in poverty. Things felt lighter, more hopeful, at least at home. But school, school was still a battlefield. I didn't fit in. I couldn't seem to find my place.

I made a few friends at secondary school, and looking back now, I wonder if they, too, were neurodivergent in their own quiet ways. But even in those friendships, I felt like the outsider. Like I didn't deserve to be there. Like I was always on the edge, hoping not to be noticed too much, not to be pushed out.

That feeling followed me into relationships. I got my first boyfriend around the age of fourteen. I didn't really fancy him, but I didn't feel I had the self-esteem to choose differently. We stayed together for about two years before I met my first serious boyfriend. Again, someone I didn't really feel drawn to, but he gave me attention. We had some good times, and that felt like enough.

Then, at eighteen, I met the father of my two eldest children. I didn't fancy him either, truthfully. I saw him as a bit childish. But I felt out of control, swept along. Now I see that was my ADHD at play, living without brakes, without that pause that lets you think *what's good for me?* I was on a kind of self-destruct path, lost in the chaos of my own mind.

At the same time, my mum had formed a new relationship with my stepfather, and I felt out of sync with everything. I'd applied to university; I'd been accepted at Exeter to study drama. Drama was where I shone back then, I guess this was also why I was so good at masking, at acting neurotypical. I'd got an A* at GCSE and a B at A-level, and I thought maybe this was my path. But my heart wasn't really in it. Not yet.

I was working at Boots Chemist, and honestly, I enjoyed it. There was something steadying about it. But the soon-to-be father of my children would come and see me there, and his attention felt like something I didn't know how to refuse. My low self-esteem led me to fall into that relationship, and soon I found myself pregnant.

Not long before I discovered I was expecting, my mum had sat us down and announced that she was pregnant too. I still remember how she felt like I'd stolen her thunder. I knew I needed to step up - to make a home, to build a life for my child. So, at eighteen, I started working full-time at

Boots, and I rented a flat with my partner. I became a parent while I was still finding my own footing in the world.

It soon became clear that the father of my child couldn't settle with just one partner. He was always seeking attention elsewhere, always needing validation from other women. I remember finding messages to other women on the computer, words he'd written about me, about us. How he wasn't happy. How I wasn't his person. How he didn't love me. My son was about one at the time, and my already fragile self-esteem took another hard hit.

I left. I went back to stay with my mum for a while, trying to piece myself back together. Eventually, I found a house in a beautiful countryside village, hoping to create a home for me and my son. But I didn't want to do it alone. I let his dad come back. I thought we'd try again, for our son, for the family I believed we were supposed to be. We decided to get married, to build a life together, to make it work. After all, we had a son. I wanted him to have siblings. I wanted that picture of a family I'd held in my heart for so long.

At twenty, I fell pregnant again, this time, it wasn't by chance. We wanted this baby. I was excited. I shared the news with my family, my colleagues at work. But at the twelve-week scan, things didn't feel right. The scan took longer than I expected, and no one said a word. I could see something on the screen, but there was no joy, no smiles. Just concern. Then the sonographer spoke: *"I'm so sorry, but there's no heartbeat."*

I waited until sixteen weeks before my body let the pregnancy go. Those weeks felt endless. When it finally happened, I was at my mum's house. My partner didn't know how to comfort me, how to be the person I needed. Nobody prepared me for what it would be like, the pain, the blood, the fear. I was twenty-one and convinced in those moments that I was dying. It changed me. It left me feeling hollow, lost, low.

But we had a wedding planned. I threw myself into it, hoping to create something happy out of the wreckage. We married. We tried to focus forward. I was working for the NHS then, and my now husband worked for the same trust. Soon after, I fell pregnant with my second son. His birth was beautiful - a home birth, one of the loveliest experiences of my life. I will always carry that memory with gratitude. When he was around one, the truth surfaced again. My husband had been seeking attention elsewhere this time with a colleague at work, the same trust we both worked at... The cycle I thought I'd escaped had found me once more.

I fell

I always fell into relationships,

Never choosing what was right for me,

I guess that's because of my low self-esteem,

And because I have ADHD,

All of my twenties felt out of control,

Like I was falling instead of living,

Getting pregnant and not thinking things through,

Not setting boundaries and always giving,

But with each encounter, we learn a new lesson,

I do believe that things happen for a reason,

Some people stay in our lives,

Some just come for a season,

My children have taught me so much in life,

I wouldn't change how some things play out,

That's one thing I would never change

I can say that without doubt.

So yes, I fell, and I didn't choose,

But I wouldn't swap with another,

Without these moments I've had in life,

I wouldn't have ever been their mother.

Chapter Four:
Breaking the Chains

This time, the relationship ended for good.

I was a single parent, now raising two young children alone. I was vulnerable. Worn down. Still searching for something I couldn't name. That's when someone from my past appeared. He said he wanted to help me.

He came to my house one day... and he never left. Before I knew it, I was in another relationship - one I hadn't asked for, one I didn't truly want. But I was too tired to fight it. He had recently been diagnosed with mental health difficulties, and my codependent heart, fragile and scarred from the past, felt responsible for him. I thought I had to care for him. I thought it was my duty to protect him. And instead of him helping me and my children, I became the one carrying the weight of it all: two young children, and now another adult who needed constant care.

Over the next eight years, I had three more children with him. Those years became some of the most emotionally draining and psychologically damaging of my life. His control over me grew slowly, subtly, until it felt complete.

He criticised everything I did. My driving. My parenting. My cooking. Even how I loaded the dishwasher.

It felt like nothing I ever did was right, not in his eyes. And because I was already worn thin, I began to believe him. I lost confidence in the smallest of things. Sometimes I didn't even feel like I had the right to speak.

He twisted my reality so often that I began to lose sight of what was true. I could stare at a purple wall, and he'd tell me it was pink - and somehow, I'd start to doubt myself.

One moment that sticks with me happened at my brother's wedding. Our daughter was still a baby then, and I had the three boys in tow. I didn't yet know about her neurodivergence, but she struggled through the day - the noise, the overstimulation, the transitions. I spent much of the ceremony walking back and forth to the toilets to settle her, feeling alone and overwhelmed. I expected understanding, even comfort, but instead, he made it worse. In the evening, he created a situation out of thin air, claiming my mum and sister had been talking about me, stirring up anxiety and paranoia. He told others I had said things I hadn't. He manipulated the moment, then waited for my reaction, and used that reaction as ammunition.

This was his pattern.

Sabotage.

He ruined holidays, weddings, and any event that might've brought me joy. If there was a day meant to celebrate me, it became a day to break me. I'd spend the next weeks being punished for how I'd "acted," my emotions used as proof that I was unstable, dramatic, unfit. Every argument we had somehow became my fault. He'd dig into the past, pull out my worst moments, and use them like weapons. Rewriting events until I questioned my own memories.

Even joyful moments were stolen. After I gave birth to our youngest, I had developed sepsis and was gravely ill in hospital. It should have been a time of deep care and concern. Instead, following this he accused me of cheating on him while I was in that hospital bed, too weak to even stand. That accusation still echoes in my mind. It wasn't just cruel - it was the final crack in an already fragile shell.

The truth is, I didn't feel safe, not even in my own home. I felt like I couldn't be myself. I couldn't speak freely. I couldn't breathe without being watched. It wasn't love. It was control.

And yet, when you're that far in, when you're worn down by years of psychological warfare, you stop recognising what's normal. You adapt. You survive. You tell yourself that this is what partnership looks like - that it's just hard right now, and things will get better.

But things didn't get better.

By 2018, I was running on fumes. I was mothering five children, emotionally isolated, mentally exhausted, and losing myself more every day. Until one day... I didn't.

I ended it.

It didn't feel dramatic - it felt like survival. I simply couldn't keep living like that. I couldn't keep modelling that relationship for my children. I couldn't keep shrinking to fit someone else's narrative of who I was.

So, I chose myself.

I chose freedom. I chose my children. I chose a different life.

And then... I chose education.

Education had always been my escape. Even as a child, I loved to learn - even if the school system didn't quite love me back. So, I returned to it with everything I had. I enrolled in an Early Childhood degree with The Open University. I studied late into the night, often with a child on my lap, or one asleep on my chest. I poured myself into every assignment, every module, every learning moment.

And I rose.

Four years later, I graduated with a first-class degree. I didn't stop there - I went on to complete a master's in psychology. With every essay, every grade, every milestone, I reclaimed a piece of myself.

Those eight years nearly broke me. But this part of my story? This part made me. I now use my voice, my insight, and my lived experience to make the system better. I stand up for what's right. I don't stay silent. I am no longer the woman who tiptoed around a partner's moods. I am the woman who broke the chain, walked out of the storm, and built something beautiful in its place.

I hope this chapter reminds you that no matter how long you've been in the dark, the light is still yours to claim. You are not what happened to you. You are what you choose to become

Narcissist

It's really hard dealing with a narcissist,
When every conversation and event, they will twist,
They deliberately try to cause a scene,
By being covert or obviously mean,
And when you get angry and express how you feel,
They make you feel crazy and pretend it's not real,
They give you attention to keep you close,
Then take it away when you need it the most,
Self-importance and superiority complex,
They'll take your words and twist them out of context,
And when they finally lose their control,
That's when they try to destroy your soul.

It's a feeling that's a little hard to explain,

It's a feeling that's a little hard to explain,
A strange sensation and emotional pain,
A grief for who I used to be,
As I change and become a better me,
Regrets of the past and sadness for she,
The one I look back on that she is me,
So innocent, young, naïve, insecure,
I've done many things, and I don't know what for.
I've given myself and laid down no boundaries,
In giving myself to others I never found me,
I wish I'd been present in time that has passed,
I feel a void now a gap that is vast,
I know I must be patient and wait and see,
If there is really someone good for me,
It gets so lonely sitting in the dark,
The gap by your side feels cold and stark,
All I want is to be loved and truly admired,
By someone who wants me and makes me feel desired,
Respect and understanding for who I truly am,
Not someone who plays me and makes me feel down,
There is a negative stigma being a single mum,
But we are superhuman here for the long run,

I'm not sure why at this time of night,
That it is alone I sit and poetry I write.

Chapter Five
Neurodivergence in Our Family

What Is Neurodivergence?

When someone is *neurotypical*, it means their brain functions in a way that aligns with what is considered the "typical" or majority way of thinking, learning, feeling, and processing the world. Neurotypical individuals often learn in "expected" ways, experience sensory input without overwhelm, and interact in ways that align with social norms.

But just as we celebrate differences on the *outside-* our cultures, appearances, and personalities - we must also recognise the diversity that exists on the *inside*. This is known as **neurodiversity**: the natural variation in how human brains are wired and how they function.

The term *neurodivergent* refers to people whose brains work differently from the typical model. This includes differences in attention, learning, sensory processing, communication, and emotional regulation. **Autism** and **ADHD** are examples of neurodivergent profiles.

Importantly, being neurodivergent is *not a deficit*. It's a different way of experiencing and interacting with the world. And those differences can come with incredible strengths, creativity, innovation, hyperfocus, empathy, and problem-solving in unique ways. As neurodiversity advocate Dr. Nick Walker explains, "Neurodiversity is not a problem to be fixed, it's a resource to be valued" (Walker, 2021).

We need all types of brains in our world. Without the gifts of neurodivergent thinkers, we wouldn't have many of the innovations, breakthroughs, and beauty we see today. From Einstein to Simone Biles, many of history's greats have been neurodivergent. Our society functions best when we embrace *all* minds, not just the ones that fit the mould.

My second-born son was the first of my children who really stood out as different, not in a bad way, just *different*. From the start, he amazed me. His memory was incredible. Before he even started school, he could recite entire books I'd read to him, word for word. By the time he started reception, he was already reading. At four and five years old, he was ahead of his peers - one of the top achievers in his class.

But while his mind was remarkable, the world wasn't always easy for him. He struggled socially and emotionally. Sensory input overwhelmed him. Birthday parties were a particular challenge; he hated going, and when we did, if he lost a game, it would end in a meltdown. He couldn't mask how hard it all felt.

In the early years of school, he held it together, just about. But by Year 4, the cracks began to show. The effort of masking became too much. The meltdowns started happening at school, not just at home. It became clear that something more was going on, something that needed understanding, not judgment.

At age nine, he was diagnosed with autism. That diagnosis changed everything. It gave us a new lens through which to see him, and ourselves. Because as we learned about autism, about neurodivergence, we started to realise something profound: neurodivergence wasn't the exception in our family. It was the thread running through so many of us.

One by one, my children received diagnoses, each with their own unique strengths and challenges, each presenting their neurodivergence in different ways. And as I stood beside them, advocating for their needs, fighting for their rights, I began to recognise those same traits in myself. The struggles, the sensitivities, the way my mind worked.

I referred myself for an ADHD assessment, and I was diagnosed at 36. They said that because my hyperactivity isn't the kind you can see, it was ADD. The hyperactivity is there though, it's the kind that lives inside my mind, racing thoughts, constant ideas, endless motion no one else could see, but I could always feel.

Following my diagnosis, I've learned to be more compassionate with myself, to stop beating myself up for the things that others seem to find so easy. My house is lived in, full of piles of things that are waiting for my attention. The clean washing often sits in a pile in my room, waiting to be put away. But that day rarely comes. Before I know it, we're pulling clothes straight from the clean pile, wearing them, and adding them back to the laundry basket to start the cycle again.

My cupboards are disorganised, except for the times when I get a burst of energy and determination, and I tidy, sort, and organise everything. For a week or two, it looks beautiful, but it never lasts. Before long, everything settles back into what I call my *organised chaos*. This is just part of living with ADHD.

It's hard to stay on top of tasks because my brain doesn't always finish or follow through. I'll go to a drawer to get something, and once I have what I need, my brain moves on, it doesn't think to close the drawer behind me. The same with cupboards, most of the time, the doors are left open because I've done the bit that mattered in that moment:

I got what I needed. I've even left the car door open before. The front door of the house. Things that would be automatic for others, my brain skips over.

I lose things on a daily basis. That's just part of the rhythm of my life, a rhythm I'm learning to accept with kindness towards myself. That diagnosis made sense of so much. It helped me understand why I'd always felt different, why I'd struggled to fit in, to focus, to slow down. And it deepened my passion, not just for supporting my own children, but for advocating, raising awareness, and helping build a world that truly accepts and understands neurodivergent people.

These poems are part of that journey. They tell the story of my discovery, my children's and of what it means to be a neurodivergent parent, raising neurodivergent children, navigating a world that too often asks us to be something we're not

ADD, they call it

ADD, they call it, but it's missing a letter,
The Drs say there's no hyperactivity in this one,
But trust me, I know better,
It's here, it's just all in my mind,
Hyperactivity of the invisible kind,
It's endless thoughts throughout the day,
Those song lyrics you heard, now here to stay,
It's overthinking every detail and every task,
It's the questions you practice before you ask,
It's the random decision to redecorate and design,
As constant ideas run through your mind,
The internal monologue, like your life has its own narrator,
The hyperactive brain the impressive creator,
The rushing thoughts that something might be wrong,
The rejection sensitivity, and again there's that song,
The imposter telling you that you're bad,
Battled by the positive thoughts to stop you feeling sad,
The endless list of things that you need to do,
It's there in the background, and it's loud too,
It's the poems that write themselves without invitation,
The mind doesn't stop it must write down this creation,
It's always busy, loud and fast in my brain,

Like a motorway with rushing cars and falling rain,
Someone says a word, and the song changes track,
Or it jogs the urge to look up a random fact,
The constant questioning of every action,
Did I say something wrong? Did I give the right reaction?
Maybe everyone hates me, maybe it's all in my head,
And all these thoughts continue even when I get into bed,
But the doctors tell me it's ADD,
Because the hyperactivity is one they cannot see.

I lose things

I lose things on a daily basis,
My keys, my phone, but the one thing I can't face is,
Losing myself to the rush of overwhelm, trauma and
torment in my brain,
When all I am really sure about myself is my name,
You see, my mind will overthink the simplest of things and
make me feel lost within a storm so bleak
It cripples my dreams, my goals, my relationships and
makes me terrified and weak,
I am just a weary, injured survivor
trying to keep myself afloat,
Yearning for a break, a breather, an answer
or a rescue boat,
I lose myself to the irrational feeling of not being good
enough,
If I can lose myself so easily, how is it possible to be
loved?
How can someone love something that can't be found?
Like a broken treasure at the bottom of the sea, I guess I'm
destined to be forever ocean-bound.

Chapter Six
The ADHD traits in me

People-Pleasing and Boundaries

Something I've come to recognise, and I know it's common for many neurodivergent people, especially those with ADHD, is a deep-rooted need to people-please, and a struggle to set boundaries. Looking back over my life, I can see how often I wasn't able to say *no*, how often I let my need to keep others happy push me into situations where I lost control over my own choices.

It's taken time, and reflection, and a lot of learning, but I've started to manage this. Still, that fear of saying *no* is something I carry, that intense worry that I'll let someone down, upset them, or be seen as difficult. But what I've come to understand is that when we don't set boundaries, we risk stepping into things that aren't meant for us. We end up drained, lost, or trapped in places that don't serve us.

Learning to say *no* is powerful. Walking away from what doesn't feel good is an act of self-care. And that feeling we sometimes try to ignore, that nudge, that discomfort, it's our intuition. I believe mine is strong. I think most of us have it, but we doubt it. We second-guess ourselves. Yet that inner voice is there for a reason. It's part of our purpose. It's meant to guide us. We just have to trust it, even when it's hard.

The Sense of Justice

Something I've touched on throughout my story - and something I've come to understand as a common trait among ADHD people - is a strong, unshakable sense of justice. That fierce, magnetic pull to speak up when something isn't right. To stand for truth, even when our voice trembles. Even when it costs us.

This isn't just anecdotal. Research has begun to explore the link between ADHD and heightened sensitivity to fairness and injustice. Psychologist Dr. William Dodson suggests that individuals with ADHD often operate with a unique emotional intensity and a deep internal compass that draws them to defend others, even to their own detriment (Dodson, 2020). In fact, many late-diagnosed ADHD adults report that as children, they were the ones sticking up for classmates, questioning unfair rules, or being labelled "too sensitive" when something felt morally wrong.

I see this pattern clearly in my own life. It's been with me for as long as I can remember, but I've felt it most deeply in my work, particularly in education. When I see things not being done properly, when policies aren't followed, when vulnerable children are left unsupported or unseen - I can't stay silent. I *have* to say something. It feels impossible not to.

But I've learned the hard way that not everyone feels this way. Some people see what's wrong but stay quiet. They choose comfort over confrontation. They allow systems to carry on as they are - even when they hurt people - because they've learned it's safer not to speak. And then there are people like me: people who speak up. People who challenge, question, push for change, and get labelled as the problem. The difficult one. The disruptive one.

As author Glennon Doyle puts it:

"The thing that is breaking your heart is the very thing you were born to help heal."

That quote lives in me. Because that's what it feels like to live with this sense of justice - like the broken bits of the world call out to you, and you can't look away.

For a long time, I internalised the idea that being "too much," "too opinionated," or "too intense" was a fault. But now I know: this fire is not a flaw. It's a gift. And it's one that many neurodivergent people carry.

This strong sense of justice is part of our wiring. A 2022 study by Hartman et al. found that individuals with ADHD scored significantly higher on measures of moral sensitivity and empathy than neurotypical controls, particularly in scenarios involving harm to others (Hartman, 2022). It's no surprise that many of us are driven into advocacy, teaching, social care, activism, or simply find ourselves constantly standing up for others.

And that's something I'm proud of now.

Neurodivergent people are often the changemakers. The ones who can't look away. The ones who ask, "Why is it like this?", and don't stop asking until something changes. We are the ones who stand our ground, who fight for fairness, who shine light where others would rather leave things in the dark.

That matters. That's important. That is part of our purpose.

Wouldn't it be nice

Wouldn't it be nice to live in ignorant bliss?
Where strong feelings and emotions they didn't exist,
Wouldn't it be nice to turn a blind eye,
To let lies and injustice just pass you by,
Wouldn't it be nice to live a simple life,
Where you're not affected by troubles and strife,
Wouldn't it be nice not to feel things so deeply?
Where you'd just ignore people acting so sneaky,
Wouldn't it be nice to be numb to it all?
To not feel those hard feelings, big or small,
Wouldn't it be nice to just stay silent,
When you see wrongdoing, aggression or violence,
Unfortunately, though I'm not born that way,
I'll have to speak up and have my say.
If I see injustice, I will speak out,
My morals are strong, so please have no doubt,
I won't just stand by and watch people be hurt,
That's not how I am, it's not what I've learnt,
I'll stand up for the person who's being mistreated,
No matter the cost, I won't be defeated,
My strong sense of justice will power me through,
Because staying silent is something I just cannot do.

Friendships and Finding My People

Throughout my life, I've had friends, but only a few people I could truly call real friends. Friends who saw me, the unmasked, authentic me, and accepted me as I am.

Socialising has always been something that drains me. My social battery empties quickly, especially around people who don't truly know me, where I feel I must mask or perform in some way. That's why friendships have often felt hard to come by, at least the kind that go beyond surface-level. I've always felt on the edge of social circles, watching, trying to fit in, but never really feeling part of the core.

What I've found is that socialising feels much easier when I have a purpose, when I'm helping someone, advocating for them, or sharing knowledge about something I care about. In those moments, the social pressure fades, and I feel more at ease.

The friendships I've formed that do feel natural have often been with people I now believe are neurodivergent too, even if they haven't been diagnosed. My best friend, for example, is almost certainly ADHD, though undiagnosed. One of my favourite colleagues over the years is likely neurodivergent as well. These are the people with whom I can have deep, meaningful conversations. People who get my sense of humour, something I rarely feel fully seen for in other groups.

I've come to realise that I naturally form bonds with like-minded people, those whose minds work in ways similar to mine. And while I value those connections deeply, I still often find myself choosing solitude over socialising. Because in solitude, I don't have to mask, I don't have to explain, I can just be.

But the truth is, not all friendships have ended with grace. Some left scars that lingered for years, and one in particular stayed with me.

While writing this book, a memory resurfaced, a message I received sixteen years ago from someone I once considered a close friend. She'd written to explain why our friendship had ended, laying out the events as she remembered them. But reading it now, through the lens of my ADHD diagnosis and lived experience, I see things so differently.

She told me I hadn't trusted her. That I had turned up uninvited to a meal, just to check up on her. But the truth is, it was a complete coincidence. I happened to be at the same restaurant with my family. No hidden motive. No plan. Just unfortunate timing. But her assumption stung. It didn't just end a friendship, it reinforced something I'd carried for years: that no matter how hard I tried, I was always misunderstood.

I've always felt on the fringes of friendships. Like, there was a social script I hadn't been handed. Even in my closest circles, I often felt a step out of sync, too intense, too emotional, too sensitive. At the time, I had no diagnosis. I didn't understand that rejection sensitivity, emotional overwhelm, and social confusion were part of my neurodivergence.

Her message painted a version of events where I was the problem. That I made things tense. That I pulled away. That I didn't reply. But what she didn't see was that I was overwhelmed. I was scared. I was masking, trying to manage emotions far bigger than I knew how to hold.

What I remember is this: feeling excluded. Watching three of them hang out without me. Feeling left out of conversations and plans. Waiting for replies that never came. Texting her when I was scared and pregnant, and receiving silence in return.

I don't write this to blame her. I understand now that we were both young, unequipped, and doing our best with what we had. But I do write it to give that younger version of myself some closure. The girl who sobbed reading that message, who thought she was broken, unlovable, always on the outside, deserves to know:

You were never the problem. You were just unrecognised. But that won't always be your story.

Friends

I have always sat on the edge looking in,
In social interactions, I didn't know where to begin,
Especially with a neurotypical,
Interactions have never been that simple,

But when I find people who think like me,
I don't have to act, I can simply be,
These are my people, these are the ones,
Where I can relax, be myself, and have fun,

So, no, I don't have lots of close friends,
But the ones I do have, I know on them I can depend,
It's not about quantity when it comes to peers,
It's quality and friendships that withstand the years.

Object Permanence and the ADHD Mind

One of the things I've come to understand about myself, something that's so common in people with ADHD, is the challenge of *object permanence*. When something is out of sight, it's truly out of mind. It's as if it stops existing altogether unless it's right in front of me.

That's why, so often, things are left out on countertops rather than tucked away neatly in cupboards. The moment I close a cupboard, it's as if it disappears. It no longer exists in my mental space. At least, that's how it feels for me.

And it isn't just objects. This applies to people, too. If I haven't seen or spoken to someone for a long time, they can slip from my day-to-day thoughts, not because I don't care, not because I don't love them, but because they're not actively in my world in that moment. This can cause difficulties in families or friendships. People might think I don't care, that I'm not making the effort. But really, it's the object permanence of ADHD at play, out of sight, out of mind, even when love and care are still there beneath the surface.

I remember once, I went to the shop, bought myself a coffee, and put it on top of the car while I loaded things in.

I got into the car, drove off, and it wasn't until later that day, when I went to make myself a coffee at home, that my brain jolted back to the memory: I'd already bought one that morning! But it had disappeared from my reality the moment it was out of sight.

These are the tricks the ADHD brain can play on you. It's part of how we experience the world, and part of what makes understanding ourselves so important.

Out of Sight

Out of sight, out of mind,
not because I don't care,
But because my world is what I see,
And when it's gone, it slips from me.

The coffee on the car roof, lost.
The face I love, but haven't crossed
In days, in weeks, I still hold dear
But feel so far when not right here.

My cupboards hide, my counters show.
My mind lets go before I know.
This is my dance, my daily fight,
to hold what's there, beyond my sight.

Sensory Processing and the ADHD Mind

When we talk about sensory processing differences, people often think of autism, but sensory challenges are common in ADHD, too. And for me, they've shaped so many of my everyday experiences, in ways I didn't fully understand until my diagnosis.

I've always had certain sensory "icks." One that's stuck with me for as long as I can remember is wooden cutlery. I can't stand the feel of it in certain contexts. And wooden lollipop sticks, I never understood how anyone could hold one in their bare hand without flinching. The dry wood against the skin feels unbearable, and the idea of that dry wood inside the mouth. It makes me feel physically sick.

Busy, noisy places overwhelm me too. I didn't know why as a child or young adult, I just knew that certain environments left me drained and tense. Loud shops, crowded spaces, places with too much visual input - they overstimulate me. I now see it for what it is: sensory overload.

Because of this, I'd often avoid large shops, choosing smaller local ones even if it meant spending more. Now, I rely heavily on delivery services like Uber and grocery apps, because stepping into a loud, busy shop feels unbearable most days.

It's not about being fussy or difficult. It's simply how my brain processes the world around me. And understanding that has helped me treat myself with more kindness.

Too Much

The world gets loud,
too bright, too near,
each sound, each shape,
too sharp, too clear.

Wood on skin,
a lollipop stick,
a simple thing
can make me sick.

The shop, the crowd,
the colours, light,
I shrink, I flinch,
I choose my quiet.

Body Image and Unlearning Shame

Body dysmorphia is common among neurodivergent people, especially women. Studies have shown that individuals with ADHD and autism are more likely to struggle with distorted body image and disordered eating behaviours. One 2021 study found that people with ADHD are **3.6 times more likely** to be diagnosed with an eating disorder, while autistic women in particular are at **significantly higher risk** of experiencing body image distress.

This has been part of my journey too. For as long as I can remember, I've focused on how my body looked, especially its size. I compared myself to others constantly. After each of my pregnancies, it became harder. The more people commented on how much weight I had lost, the more I felt like being smaller was what I was *meant* to be doing. That praise became addictive. It fed the belief that shrinking was the goal.

At times, I would starve myself. I'd go on extreme diets, punishing routines, desperate to take up less space. I didn't understand that what I really needed was acceptance, not from others, but from myself.

Unlearning that "skinny equals worthy" mindset has taken work. Real work. But I've come to understand that a healthy body isn't necessarily a slim one. A healthy body is a *nourished* one. A loved one. A body I can live in, breathe in, feel safe in.

This next poem reflects that journey - the pain, the pressure, and the reclaiming of my body as my own.

Worth

Am I worth any less because I have curves?
Does the number on the scale or the size of my body define my worth?
Is my worth as a mother, friend or partner any less?
Because of the size of the label on my dress,
Do the curves that move like nature's intention,
Mean the work that I do is not worth a mention,
Does the body that carried and birthed human life,
Have to be shrunk and even put under a knife?
If my body moves, is nourished, and loved,
Why can't that just be enough?
Why does the media tell us we must be thinner?
Take a pill, count calories or even skip dinner,
Why must we fast, starve and obsess?
Just to reduce the number inside of that dress,
Or should we embrace nature's beauty, be it curvy, thick thighs, small or big booty,
Why must we shrink ourselves for an ideal?
To try to match the standards that aren't even real.
My body is soft, it moves, and it flows,
and with everything in nature, it changes and grows.

The Fraud in the Mirror – Impostor Syndrome

Imposter syndrome has followed me like a shadow, persistent, insidious, and loudest when I achieve the most. Despite a first-class degree and a master's that I poured my whole self into, there's still this nagging voice that whispers, *You probably fluked it.* How could I possibly have earned that? How could someone like me, juggling single parenthood, neurodivergence, and survival, have managed to succeed?

This isn't just a fleeting insecurity - it runs deeper. It feels like I'm constantly trying to convince the world I'm capable, while quietly doubting myself every step of the way. It's as though I'm wearing a mask that I'm terrified might slip. And yet, I now know I'm far from alone in this.

Research confirms that impostor syndrome is especially prevalent in neurodivergent individuals like me. Studies show that people with ADHD and autism are more likely to experience chronic self-doubt and feelings of fraudulence, even in the face of clear success. One study describes how autistic individuals, especially those diagnosed later in life, often question their legitimacy, not only in their achievements but in their very identity as neurodivergent people. This phenomenon, often called "autistic impostor syndrome," is so common that it's considered a hallmark of late diagnosis (Embrace Autism, 2022).

For those with ADHD, the constant experience of executive function struggles, forgetfulness, emotional dysregulation, disorganisation, can make success feel accidental or undeserved. As ADHD coach Eric Tivers explains, people with ADHD often internalise years of failure and negative feedback, which fuels distorted beliefs about competence (Tivers, 2020). We may excel in bursts, but because it feels so chaotic or inconsistent, we tell ourselves it doesn't count.

In my case, this internal narrative of not being "enough" is tangled with low self-esteem and decades of masking. I've worked so hard to keep up appearances, emotionally, academically, even physically, that when something good happens, it feels like a clerical error in the universe. According to Alison Shamir (2023), imposter syndrome in neurodivergent women is further compounded by rejection sensitivity, perfectionism, and a lifelong sense of "otherness", a potent cocktail that leaves us silently screaming: *Am I really good enough to be here?*

I now understand that these feelings aren't signs of failure - they're symptoms of living in a world that hasn't been designed for brains like mine. Every achievement I've earned was not luck or illusion. It was effort, passion, persistence, and more than anything, survival. And slowly, I'm learning that surviving and succeeding at the same time isn't fraud. It's resilience.

Impostor

I live my life feeling like I'm an impostor, a fake,
I wonder how many more times it will take,
For people to realise I'm not all that they think of me,
And yes, I achieved a first-class degree
But perhaps that was just luck or a fluke,
Is it just something everyone can do?
Oh, and my master's degree with merit,
But still, I'm an impostor, I can't take credit,
And when people give me a compliment or praise,
I want to hide or for them to just go away,
As I shake my head and say no, I'm not that,
It can't be true, you don't know all the facts,
At work, when people tell me I'm great,
I say no, I just feel like a fake.
And when I'm creative and I write out my words,
And people tell me that their best that they've heard,
I just shake my head and say no, it's not true,
I just think it's something anyone could do,
I'm consumed by the impostor in me,
Because I truly don't see what the other see.

Empathy, Intuition, and the ADHD Mind

One of the most misunderstood aspects of ADHD is the emotional intensity that often comes with it. For me, this intensity shows up as deep empathy - so deep that sometimes it feels like I'm *wearing* someone else's emotions. If I see someone crying, I can't help but feel it in my own chest. Their pain becomes my pain. It's not just sympathy - it's something raw, visceral, and consuming. This isn't uncommon for people with ADHD. While some studies suggest that "affective empathy" (the ability to feel another's emotions) may vary, our "cognitive empathy" (the ability to understand another's emotional state) often remains strong (Groen et al., 2018; Done ADHD, 2023). Dr. Edward Hallowell, a leading expert on ADHD, describes people with the condition as possessing a heightened emotional sensitivity, often absorbing the emotional climate around them like a sponge (Hallowell, 2021).

But alongside this empathy comes something else: intuition. A kind of knowing that doesn't always make logical sense but turns out to be right more often than not. I've always had a sense about people - their energy, their intentions, even the things they're not saying out loud. I can walk into a room and feel tension without a word being spoken. I can sense when someone is holding back tears or pretending to be okay. This intuitive knowing has guided me throughout my life, though, I'll admit, there have been times it's also made me overly suspicious or emotionally reactive.

Emerging neuroscience suggests that the ADHD brain has a natural strength in "broad associative processing" - linking ideas, patterns, and feelings in nonlinear ways, often through the right hemisphere of the brain, which excels at emotional and intuitive processing (SimplyWellbeing, 2022). Our brains can rapidly interpret subtle cues like body language, tone, and energy shifts, giving us what feels like a sixth sense. Some researchers and advocates call this a superpower of the ADHD mind (The Wave Clinic, 2023). However, it can also become overwhelming, especially when combined with Rejection sensitivity.

I've had to learn how to care for myself within this sensitivity, how to ground, breathe, and protect my energy when I feel too much. My empathy and intuition are part of my identity. They are gifts, but only when I honour my own boundaries too. It's taken time, but I've come to see that this part of me - the emotional, intuitive, deeply feeling part - isn't something broken. It's something beautiful.

Sometimes

Sometimes I wish I didn't think as deeply as I do,
Could switch off my brain and sleep the whole night through.
But as much as my mind is unique and can shine so bright,
It tends to overthink, especially at night.

In creep the doubts, the feelings I can't outrun,
Not just my own, but the pain of everyone.
If someone is hurting, I feel it inside,
Their tears become mine - no place to hide.

Perhaps I'll play a podcast or put on a happy song,
Try to drown the noise that's been echoing so long.
I want to hush the heartache, the chaos in my head,
Just close my eyes, find peace, get some rest instead.

These feelings run deep - they're hard to contain,
Empathy like waves, washing through my brain.
And though it's exhausting, I know it's part of me,
This tender heart, this intensity - my wired empathy.

Social anxiety and depression

Socialising has always been difficult for me. As I've already described, fitting in never came naturally. I remember when my children were babies and I'd take them to toddler groups, and I'd overthink everything. What I was wearing. How I appeared. How I was being perceived. Every glance, every word, every silence. It left me drained, overwhelmed, and exhausted.

Now I understand that this was because of my neurodivergence. For many women with ADHD, social situations can be mentally exhausting. The constant internal narrative - *Am I saying too much? Am I too much? Not enough?* - isn't just anxiety; it's the result of years of masking and navigating a world not designed for our brains.

I used to come home from those groups feeling unwell, physically and emotionally. How could something so simple, something other parents seemed to find so easy, feel so hard for me? But I didn't know at the time. I wasn't diagnosed. So, I blamed myself. I told myself I was the problem. That self-blame chipped away at my self-esteem, leaving me feeling low and lost.

Before my ADHD diagnosis, I had been given other labels - anxiety, depression -and prescribed antidepressants.

But now I can see that what was often described as "depression" was actually burnout. Burnout from trying so hard to fit in. From overdoing everything. From never having the time or space to truly rest and recharge. A 2022 study published in *BMJ Mental Health* noted that "women with ADHD are often misdiagnosed with mood disorders, such as depression or anxiety, before their neurodivergence is identified" (Young et al., 2022).

What I needed wasn't to be medicated for a mislabelled condition. I needed understanding. I needed permission to pause. To breathe. To recover.

During my master's studies, I chose to focus my research on something that had touched my life so deeply: the impact of late ADHD diagnosis on women. One of the patterns that stood out was just how often women are misdiagnosed, with anxiety, with depression, even with bipolar disorder, when undiagnosed neurodivergence lies beneath it all. Research from the ADHD Foundation confirms that girls and women are frequently overlooked because they "present differently" - often internalising rather than externalising symptoms - and are diagnosed, on average, **four to five years later than boys** (ADHD Foundation, 2021).

I was diagnosed at 36. My mum, only recently, at over 60. The impact of these late diagnoses is profound on mental health, on self-worth, on our entire sense of who we are. A 2021 qualitative study found that many women experience a complete "reframing of self" following diagnosis, finally understanding the lifelong struggles they'd previously attributed to personal failure (Ramsay & Rostain, 2021).

And that's why I speak, I write, I advocate, because it shouldn't take so long for neurodivergent women to be seen. We shouldn't have to carry shame for simply existing differently.

Burnout or Depression

It's like a crushing feeling that stops you in your tracks,
A sharp stabbing through your chest into your back,
So much is rushing through your mind,
Are you good enough, are you being kind?
Feel like a failure of a mother, but you know there is no other,
Irritable and angry, you get so snappy,
Are you ruining their lives and making them unhappy?
You're pushed to the edge and have no more to give,
You don't want to take for granted the life you could live,
But you can't stop the feelings that come from within,
You're not good enough and feel like you've sinned,
You try your hardest every single day but still get it wrong in every way!......
I put on a smile and say that I'm fine
And people think I'm positive all of the time,
They don't know how I do it and keep so upbeat,
Welcome to my depression, someone you're yet to meet,
It's a numbness throughout that fills you with dread,
You wake in the morning barely slept in the bed,
All you want is to shut down and stay asleep,
But there are children to feed and a house to keep.
Depression.

Social Anxiety

Social life has never been easy for me,
Even though a confident face is what you might see.
My brain is overthinking - non-stop, no end,
Even when I'm spending time with friends.

And it doesn't stop when the moment is done -
It lingers, whispers: *Was I too much? Was I no fun?*
It spirals on - *Am I good enough?*
Oh, how it burns,
This stuff is tough.

It drains me dry, leaves me spent,
And I don't understand where the energy went.
Why isn't it like this for everyone else?
Is it low self-esteem?
Is it ADHD - or just how I've always felt?

Is that why connection feels so hard for me?

The Gift of Hyperfocus

One of the more surprising gifts from my ADHD brain is hyperfocus. Despite the word "deficit" in ADHD, I've found myself able to concentrate with incredible intensity on subjects that interest me, sometimes for hours, completely oblivious to the world around me.

When I'm locked into something I care about, like writing this book, time disappears. Hours can pass, and I won't even notice. The same thing happens when I'm hit with a burst of energy to redecorate or start a DIY project; I'll become totally immersed, forgetting to eat, rest, or check my phone. These hyperfocus episodes aren't constant, but when they come, they come with force.

This isn't just a personal quirk; it's a recognised trait of ADHD. According to the Attention Deficit Disorder Association, hyperfocus is "a state of intense and prolonged concentration on a subject or activity" that is highly stimulating or rewarding (ADD.org, 2023). Neuroscientific research has also confirmed that adults with ADHD traits are significantly more likely to experience hyperfocus compared to neurotypical individuals, especially when engaged in tasks that offer instant feedback or emotional satisfaction (Zhang et al., 2020).

It's somewhat ironic. The condition is named for an attention *deficit*, yet I can pay *incredible* attention to things that capture my interest. The challenge is with tasks that don't engage me, then my focus slips away almost instantly. At school, for example, I struggled with maths and other subjects that didn't hold my attention. I couldn't sit still, couldn't concentrate, and so I was often labelled as a daydreamer or not working hard enough. It gave the impression that I wasn't very bright.

But that wasn't true. When I was given space to explore subjects I *did* care about, especially during my degree and master's studies, I could pour myself into the work completely. I would hyperfocus for hours, refining my assignments to near perfection. I didn't want to stop. In those moments, time didn't seem to exist. Research suggests this experience is tied to how the ADHD brain is wired for reward sensitivity; tasks that trigger dopamine release, like learning something meaningful, can spark intense cognitive engagement (Barkley, 2015).

This capacity to hyperfocus has played a huge part in my academic success. It's what enabled me to go from struggling to read and write as a child to graduating with a first-class degree in Early Childhood and a master's with merit in psychology. I'm living proof that struggling in traditional education doesn't mean you lack intelligence - it just means you learn differently.

Attention Deficit?

The title deceives,
You can't pay attention,
That's what the world believes.
But oh, how wrong that view can be,
When a spark of interest
Takes hold of me.

I can't take a break, can't step away,
It's all-consuming,
Time slips away.
Hours lost in laser focus,
Be it writing, crafting, or DIY,
My attention?
Believe me, I've got it, sky high.

It's fixed on a project, a mission, a plan,
Nothing will stop me,
Not even I can.
Ideas, designs, answers I seek,
With passion that burns,
And a mind that won't sleep.

So, trust me when I say,
It's not a deficit that I display.
I spend my nights and every day,
Hyper focused, no off switch,
Just pure, unfiltered
Attention

Zoning Out: The Art of Going Nowhere (Fast)

One of the more mysterious traits of my ADHD brain is zoning out. From the outside, it just looks like I'm staring into space, mid-blink, possibly contemplating the meaning of life. But inside, my brain has clicked "Do Not Disturb" and wandered into an internal brainstorm about everything from childhood trauma to whether I remembered to lock the front door (or even close it).

This isn't laziness, rudeness, or intentional ignorance; it's linked to the **inattentive presentation of ADHD**. It's like your body is here, but your mind is... buffering. I can zone out mid-conversation, while doing the dishes, or worst of all, *while driving*. Now, before you panic, let me explain.

When I drive, my body knows what to do. That's because driving is what's known in psychology as an **automatic process**. Once a task is overlearned and routine, like brushing your teeth or tying your shoelaces, it requires very little conscious effort to execute. This is known as **automaticity** (Shiffrin & Schneider, 1977). So even when I'm zoned out, my motor system still handles the mechanics of driving. Steering, braking, and checking mirrors all still happen. But it's *where* I'm going that often gets... lost in transit.

Just yesterday, I was driving down the A12 to get back to Colchester, a journey I've done countless times. Somewhere between the turnoff and my rewriting half a chapter in my head, I missed the exit completely. It wasn't until I saw a road sign for *Suffolk*, yes, an *entire other county*, that I realised: Ah. I've done it again.

This is more than just a distraction; it's deeply tied to how the ADHD brain regulates attention. Many of us with ADHD experience frequent activation of the **default mode network (DMN),** a brain network associated with internal thoughts, daydreaming, and self-referential processing (Buckner, Andrews-Hanna & Schacter, 2008). In neurotypical brains, the DMN typically "switches off" when you're focusing on a task. But in ADHD, it tends to remain active, or switches on too easily, pulling attention away from the external world and into internal wanderings.

So, while I was physically driving, my brain was halfway through narrating a paragraph about trauma and resilience. My car was heading to Colchester. My mind? On a literary TED Talk.

This mismatch between attention and action is a classic symptom of **executive dysfunction**, another hallmark of ADHD. Our executive functions, which help with things like planning, sustaining attention, switching tasks, and self-monitoring, often struggle to prioritise what's *most* important in the moment. So instead of focusing on turn-offs and road signs, my brain prioritised emotionally intense internal content. (Of course it did. That's *much* more stimulating.)

I've walked into rooms and completely forgotten why I'm there. I've zoned out at till checkouts, in queues, during conversations, I've probably nodded my way through at least three emotionally loaded stories while thinking about what to cook for dinner, or an email I need to send or respond to. Not because I don't care, but because my brain is always toggling between now and next, between presence and preoccupation.

Zoning out isn't me being absent. It's me being *too present*, just not here. I'm fully immersed... just not in the current reality. And while it's mildly alarming to end up in the wrong county, I've learned to find humour in it too. Because at the end of the day, that's part of my ADHD: Unexpected detours, rogue thoughts, and moments where my body's on autopilot but your soul is off writing poetry in another postcode.

Chapter Seven
The Missing Weeks - Living with PMDD

From the age of 18 to 35, I was either pregnant or breastfeeding. Seven pregnancies in total - five of which brought me the greatest joys of my life, my children. I breastfed each one, starting with 14 months for my eldest, and gradually extending with each baby. By the time I reached my youngest, she was still breastfeeding well past two and a half years old.

In some ways, I think this constant stream of pregnancies and breastfeeding acted like a hormonal shield. I didn't realise it at the time, but I was living in a near-continuous state of hormonal protection - my brain bathed in natural boosts of serotonin, oxytocin, and the stabilising rhythms of pregnancy and breastfeeding. But when that cycle ended - when I finally stopped breastfeeding- I noticed something was deeply wrong.

Each month, in the days before my period, I would spiral. This wasn't just PMT. This was deeper, darker. A fog of depression would roll in, exhaustion, irritability, emotional overwhelm, and a sense of despair that made me want to give up everything. I would withdraw. Isolate.

Question everything. And then, like clockwork, it would lift once my period began, only for the cycle to begin again.

Eventually, I discovered a name for what I was experiencing: PMDD - Premenstrual Dysphoric Disorder.

PMDD affects an estimated 5–8% of women and is characterised by severe emotional and physical symptoms that occur in the luteal phase (the week or so before menstruation) and resolve shortly after menstruation begins. It's not caused by abnormal hormone levels, but rather by an increased sensitivity to the normal hormonal fluctuations that occur during the menstrual cycle.

For individuals with ADHD, this sensitivity is often magnified. Recent studies suggest that hormonal changes - especially drops in estrogen and progesterone - can significantly affect dopamine and serotonin regulation, which are already dysregulated in ADHD brains.

"Women with ADHD are more likely to experience PMDD and other mood disturbances linked to the menstrual cycle." - Quinn & Madhoo, 2014, Journal of Clinical Psychiatry.

Estrogen plays a key role in boosting serotonin, the "feel-good" neurotransmitter. During breastfeeding, prolactin and oxytocin naturally elevate mood and reduce anxiety. When breastfeeding ends, that hormonal support drops, potentially triggering or worsening PMDD symptoms.

Moreover, ADHD brains are particularly sensitive to changes in dopamine and serotonin, making women more vulnerable to the mood volatility caused by hormonal shifts.

Understanding PMDD gave me language. It gave me context. I wasn't broken - I was hormonally sensitive, neurodivergent, and responding in a perfectly logical way to chemical shifts in my body.

But knowing doesn't always make it easier.

Every month, I still brace myself for that week. The "lost week," I call it. The week when the darkness comes. Where the thoughts creep in. Where survival means slowing down, doing less, leaning on tools I've learned to build - journaling, gentle movement, supplements, structure, and grace.

And then it passes. The world resets. But I'm left to rebuild from the chaos once more.

Chapter 8
Work That Moves Me

When my second-born son was first diagnosed with autism, it changed everything. What started as a personal journey soon became a professional calling. As more of my children were identified as neurodivergent, I immersed myself in understanding the education system, not just for them, but for families like mine who were being overlooked, misunderstood, and left behind.

While studying, I found myself stepping into the role of an advocate. I began helping other parents navigate the complex processes of securing Education, Health and Care Plans (EHCPs), applying for Disability Living Allowance (DLA), and preparing for tribunal hearings. It wasn't easy work, but it felt natural. In fact, it was energising. My ADHD brain thrived on the challenge, the urgency, the purpose. I could hyperfocus for hours on a case, digging deep into legislation, writing appeals, and preparing evidence with meticulous attention to detail. I wasn't just working - I was driven.

Advocacy gave me something I'd never really felt in the workplace before: alignment. It illuminated every part of my brain. I found comfort in helping others, but more than that, I found focus. And for someone with ADHD, that's a rare and golden thing.

Eventually, my work expanded. I began working with the local authority, raising awareness of Special Educational Needs and Disabilities (SEND) in schools. Once again, the role aligned with my passions and interests. I was able to use my voice and lived experience to improve understanding, shift attitudes, and advocate from the inside out. And again, my neurodivergence helped me, not hindered me. My energy, my creativity, my ability to speak up and see things differently - all became assets in this setting.

One thing I've learned through these roles is that I could never survive in a standard 9-to-5, desk-bound job. My brain just isn't wired for that. ADHD requires stimulation, variety, and movement. I need work that excites me - work that matters, that I can hyperfocus on, that allows me to be myself. Research backs this up: people with ADHD often thrive in environments that offer autonomy, novelty, and alignment with personal interests (White & Shah, 2006). The more engaged we are, the more likely we are to sustain attention and succeed.

For me, the key to a successful career hasn't been following a conventional path - it's been following my passions. And for those of us with ADHD, that's more than just advice. It's essential. When we are allowed to work in ways that complement how our brains function, we don't just cope - we thrive.

From Advocate to Psychologist in the Making

As my confidence in advocacy grew, so did something else, an inner calling I couldn't ignore. I started to realise that the work I was doing wasn't just about navigating systems. It was about understanding people. Understanding behaviour. Understanding the "why" behind the way children learn, react, regulate, and connect.

Psychology had always intrigued me, and I had been inspired by Educational Psychologists on my journey, but now it felt personal. I saw my children's minds, not just through the lens of diagnoses and education plans, but through curiosity and care. I wanted to know more - not just to help them, but to support others who felt lost, labelled, or unheard.

Balancing study with single parenthood, neurodivergence, and work wasn't easy. There were days when I doubted myself, when the impostor syndrome crept in and whispered, *You don't belong here. You're not academic enough. You're just a mum who's winging it.* But every assignment I completed, every concept I mastered, pushed that voice a little further into the background.

Once again, my ADHD became my superpower. I could hyperfocus for hours on my coursework. I'd read entire journals in one sitting, obsessively research areas that piqued my interest, and apply theory to real-world experiences I'd lived through a hundred times. The more I studied, the more I saw how much of psychology still overlooked neurodivergent voices - especially those of mothers, carers, and working-class women. And I wanted to change that.

That's when I knew. I didn't just want to understand psychology - I wanted to help shape it. I wanted to challenge the old narratives and centre the voices of those who are so often left out. I wanted to be the kind of psychologist who sees the whole person, not just the presentation. Who listens not just to data, but to stories.

My goal now is to bring everything I've lived, everything I've studied, and everything I've fought for into the field of educational psychology. Not just as a profession, but as a mission.

Because if there's one thing my journey has taught me, it's this: people like me - neurodivergent, emotionally driven, messy, passionate, imperfect - don't just deserve a seat at the table.

We belong at the head of it.

Chapter Nine
Navigating the System

Navigating the education system as a parent of children with special educational needs (SEN) taught me more than any degree ever could. I hyper-focused on SEND law, completed a SEN law qualification, driven by urgency, by love, by necessity. I learned my children's legal rights to an education because no one was going to fight for them if I didn't.

It quickly became clear that the system is broken. Failing. It cannot meet even the most basic needs of children like mine. From the very beginning, it was a battle to get my son an Education, Health and Care Plan (EHCP) - despite him clearly being unable to cope in a mainstream environment. He was academically able, and that, in the eyes of the system, seemed to disqualify him from the support he needed.

We were told he was "too able" for a special school. The first alternative provision offered was an SEMH school - an hour away from home. But his primary need wasn't SEMH. It was Autism. His emotional and behavioural challenges stemmed directly from being unsupported, misunderstood, and traumatised by a mainstream system that was never built with children like him in mind.

Since then, they've tried all kinds of placements. All kinds of boxes. And every one of them failed. Because, in truth, there is *nowhere* he fits.

Fighting for something that doesn't exist

Fighting for something that doesn't exist,
Because there's nowhere in education that your child fits.
That's not on them, it's down to the system,
Because when they planned schools,
They must have missed them,
Thousands of children, intellectually bright,
But the mainstream education sends them into fight or flight.
It's not right for all, and the send schools are full.
And for some on the spectrum, send schools aren't right at all,
There's a gap in the system, a large gaping hole,
And it's failing our children who are left out in the cold,
You fight for help with sweat and tears,
You face all the challenges and overcome all the fears,
The EHCP granted you think there's light at the end,
But sorry, they say "we can't cater for your SEND"
Your grades are too high, and you can't go to that school.
No mainstreams not right, you won't manage at all,
So, where do we go, We plead and we say,
We can offer a tutor for 3 hours a day?
But what will they do when they are home?

With no friends to talk to and they are isolated alone,
So, you fight some more, asking for help and support,
And the years go by, and your child's left untaught,
Mountains of paperwork, appointments and lists,
Meetings and discussions, but nothing really exists,
Not for this group left with no education,
This system is a sorry disgrace to our nation,
Look back at the hundreds of emails sent,
The appointment letters were hours you spent,
Just fighting and fighting, but what for?
Because there's no fight left anymore,
There is no school that fits, and the system failed.

So, you pick up the pieces and put on a brave face.
Learning is a journey, and it's not a race.
I'll support my child where the system couldn't,
I'll show them the way where the system wouldn't,
I'll end the fight for something that doesn't exist,
Listen to my child and do as they wish,
For that's the way to only get them calm,
To keep them happy and safe from harm,
One day they will study, work and succeed,
Because they've learnt from me all that they need.

Assumptions

You can make your assumptions,

You can give it a guess,

But it's not what you see,

And I have to confess,

My son has an invisible disability,

And no one knows him better than me,

The panic, the fear, confusion and stress,

All because he's been asked to get dressed,

No, he's not stubborn or being a brat,

You see, it's all a bit deeper than that,

His senses are overloaded so much,

He can't stand the smell, the sound or the touch,

He might explode with aggression and fear,

He will run away if you even come near,

He just needs some space, please don't crowd.

All he hears from your words is noise that's too loud,

Any demand will start a panic attack.

He will become scared and start to hit back,

No, it's not something that you can cure,

If you don't understand, please research a bit more.

Please don't change a plan without warning,

This can cause meltdowns that last till the next morning,

It may be scary for your child to see,

But it's scarier for him, believe you me,
All he wants is love and some understanding,
As his Mum, I will fight and always stand by him.

School Mornings

You wake them in the morning,
Their tummy feels with dread,
You need to get them up,
But they want to stay in bed,
Their little mind starts worrying,
As the day begins to dawn,
As a mum, you start hurrying,
'They can't be late for school',
But the system needs fixing,
It's not working for all,
Can't get them to eat breakfast
They don't want to go to school,
The environment is too much,
For all their sensory needs,
They can't stand the smell or touch,
'Don't send me in', they plead,
You tell the teachers of the fear,
You ask them to understand,
"They're fine when they're here"
They say, as they take them by the hand,
Children walk in compliant,
to mask throughout the day,

They come home defiant,
Don't send me again, they say,
Yet parents get fined
For keeping them home,
Even when it's best for their mind,
It's not an absence they condone,
And so it goes on,
And the parents get the blame,
And the school system continues,
Failing children and staying the same.

Party

Today I watched and saw the worry in your eyes,
Although you tried so hard,
You couldn't put on your disguise.
I see the other children all laughing having fun,
But you can't leave my side because of autism,
Afterwards, you told me the things that you would say
If autism wasn't there and didn't get in your way.
It's moments like that, a party in the day,
That really makes me realise how hard it is for you to play.
The environment is overwhelming,
There is noise, and it's not fair.
You were so excited to go and wanted me to do your hair,
You got into your dress,
And you are brave and put on a smile.
But when we got to the party, you held on tight all the while.

Neurodivergence Awareness Week

Neurodivergence Awareness Week,
But it's more than awareness that we seek,
It's acceptance, understanding and seeing our powers,
The creative thinkers, the daydreamers,
the hyper-focusing for hours,
It's understanding that our brains don't work the same as neurotypical,
But it's not black and white, it's not that simple,
Every neurodivergent person experiences the world differently,
Some of us with autism, tics, or ADHD,
Neurodiversity is a vast spectrum,
And we need to learn about people's experiences and respect them,
Yes, there are struggles as we navigate a neurotypical society,
Where neurodivergence has not been a priority,
But we must make a change,
Recognise all brains,
And the unique abilities that come with being different, not the same,

We need to understand what it means when our brains are different,
So, people don't think neurodivergence is something it isn't,
Some people have sensory differences, touch, sight, taste, smell and sound.
They might get overwhelmed with smells and noise all around,
So, have some understanding and listen to the neurodivergent community,
So that we can live in perfect and happy unity,
We are all different on the outside of our being,
But there's a difference in our brains that people aren't seeing,
Diversity is important, and neurodiversity is too.
If we didn't have all types of brains, we would be limited in what we can do,
No technology, inventions or big ideas,
Because it's taken all types of brains to develop these over the years,
Please listen, please accept please do not judge,
Raise awareness and understanding so we can be us.

Childs Mental Health

There's a mental health crisis among our young people,
They need to get some help, but it isn't that simple.
In a country that's got a staggering wealth,
Why isn't a priority child's mental health?
A Referral to CAMHS that just gets rejected
Some get through, but many aren't selected,
Despite self-harm and depression, it seems,
They don't meet the criteria, whatever that means.
Signposted to other organisations,
But that comes with it's own trepidations,
You reach the end of a waiting list,
They must attend group work, they insist,
But this is a child who will not engage,
Being in a group feels them with rage!

Chapter 10

Born to Mother

Motherhood has been a constant in my life. I've been a parent for all of my adult life; it defines who I am. From the moment I carried my first baby, something deep and natural awakened in me. Carrying my children, giving birth to them, breastfeeding, nurturing, co-sleeping, all these things felt intuitive. I've never doubted my ability to love and nurture my children. I was the child who used to look after the younger ones at school or in the family. Being a mum felt like my purpose.

But stepping outside the confines of our home into society, that's where it became difficult.

The world has a lot of opinions about what "good" parenting should look like, especially when you're parenting neurodivergent children. The parenting that my children needed didn't always match the expectations of others, and I found myself constantly judged.

Parenting with ADHD is a unique experience. The parts of parenting that society sees as basic, like organising school admin, remembering appointments, filling out reading diaries, staying on top of uniforms and socks, are the parts that challenge me the most. It's not that I don't care. It's that my brain doesn't prioritise those tasks naturally. I once decided to only buy one colour of socks for everyone in the house because I could never keep matching pairs together. My house might not be perfectly organised, but it is full of love.

There are days when I feel far from perfect. Days when I feel like I'm failing or letting my children down. ADHD means I get overstimulated. Sometimes I just need five minutes of quiet, and I can't get it. That pressure builds. There are moments I might snap or cry. But I've learned, and I teach my children, that it's okay to be human. Those feelings are valid. That, even adults, need to apologise sometimes.

One thing I always promised myself: if I ever raise my voice or get overwhelmed, I will apologise. Because respect doesn't just go one way. Children deserve it too.

Parenting my son, who was diagnosed with autism and has a PDA profile, taught me even more. With him, I had to unlearn everything I thought I knew about discipline. Traditional parenting didn't work. He didn't respond to consequences or rules. He responded to understanding, connection, and creativity. That took courage, especially when my partner at the time would say I was "too soft." He'd tell me I needed to be firmer, harsher.

But I knew in my bones that wasn't the way.

He once told me I was too protective. That I always had my "sword and shield" out for my children. And he was right. I do. I always will.

Because the truth is, the world isn't always kind to our children. Especially not neurodivergent ones. So yes, I will protect them with every part of me: with my soul, my voice, my fight. There is no such thing as too much protection when it comes to your children.

Parenting children, on my own, is beautiful and brutal in equal measure. It is *relentless*. It is raw. It is loud. It never stops. And there is no pause button.

I can't remember the last time I went to the toilet in peace. Not once. Not ever. It's like the very sound of me locking the bathroom door sends out some invisible signal to all the children: *Mum has entered the bathroom. Commence the crisis.*

And they don't knock. Oh no. They've mastered the ancient art of unlocking the door from the outside with a coin. It's impressive, really.

There I am, trying to take a relaxing bath, candles lit, bubbles foaming, and one of them strolls in mid-sentence, sits down like it's a therapy session, and starts asking deep life questions… all while casually poking my stomach.

"Why's your belly jiggly when you move, Mum?" Because life, darling.

One of them once broke a brand-new TV by spinning a cat toy ninja-style straight into the screen. That's the kind of chaos we live with. Sometimes it's funny, sometimes it's infuriating, sometimes it's both at once.

Maybe that's why I stay up until 1 or 2 a.m. most nights. Not because I want to, but because those are the only hours that belong solely to me. The only time the house is still, and I can *hear myself think*. That's when I write. That's when I reclaim a little piece of myself.

Because the truth is, parenting with ADHD adds layers of complexity, but it also adds magic.

I'm creative. Intuitive. Deeply empathetic. I see the world differently, and so do my children. Together, we're not trying to fit into a mould. We're building a life that works for *us*.

Parenting with ADHD means navigating life with a brain that struggles with consistency, memory, and executive function, often paired with deep-rooted shame from a lifetime of feeling "not good enough." Studies have shown that parents with ADHD experience more parenting stress, particularly in managing household tasks, responding to child behaviour, and maintaining routines (Chronis-

Tuscano et al., 2008). These challenges are real, but they don't make us lesser parents. They simply mean we parent differently.

For the last six years, I've been doing this alone. Single parenting neurodivergent children. I carry the weight of it all. I show up even when I'm falling apart. It is exhausting. It is consuming. It's 24/7, with no sick days, no annual leave, no "me time" unless I steal it back in the early hours.
And still, I wouldn't change it for the world.

Because in the chaos, there is joy. In the mess, there is meaning. And in the middle of everything, when the house is finally quiet and I'm lying next to one of them as they drift off to sleep, there is peace.

My children are my calm in the storm. My grounding force in a whirlwind life. They have shaped me into the woman I am today. Fierce. Tender. Resilient. Real.

In many ways, our neurodivergence is our superpower. We parent with intensity, creativity, humour, passion, and empathy. We feel deeply. And our children feel deeply loved. That counts. That matters.

Mother's Mantra:

"I am not perfect. I am present. I may lose my temper, forget the forms, or cry in the kitchen - but I will always show up with love, with apology, and with my sword and shield.

Hold On to Each Stage

You hold them in your arms - those precious little moments,
They tell you how fast time will go,
And that soon, that baby will be grown.

"Cherish every second," they gently say,
"Hold on to each smile before it slips away."
Because every stage, though tiring and tough,
Will one day feel like it wasn't enough.

The midnight feeds, the sleepy cries,
The way they look into your eyes.
The little hands that reach for you,
The firsts you'll witness, the tears you'll soothe.

It all moves faster than we know,
In the blink of an eye, they're ready to go.
So, pause, breathe in, and hold them tight,
For these are the days that will feel like light.

Not every moment will be soft and sweet,
But even the chaos is love on repeat.

So, when the days blur and you're feeling your age,
 Just remember - there's magic in every stage.

Single Mum

Tired, drained, sick or ill,
A single Mum will be there still,
She has no choice but to carry on,
The hours seem slow, and the days are long,
But the love she has remains untouched,
There's not a soul who has loved this much,
She will rise when she should fall
She has no choice but to do it ALL
Through pain, hurt, exhaustion and tears,
She will show up despite her fears,
School runs, appointments, holidays and clubs,
From swimming, cadets, scouts and cubs,
She's the cheerleader standing strong,
She will pick up the pieces if it all goes wrong,
She'll wipe their tears and hold them tight,
She is there through day and night,
She gets double the love and double the fun,
But there's no day's rest for a single Mum.

School Run

Wake them up as gently as you can,
Try to start the day positively, that's the plan.
Come on, darlings, it's time to get ready.
But they pull up the covers,
Now starts the dread of all parents and mothers,
Get them dressed and ready for the day,
Hope that we make it on time, we pray,
But it seems these children have another plan,
As they dawdle and move slower than anything known to man,
But the socks don't feel right, and you can't find a shoe.
Then the youngest decides she needs a last-minute poo,
Hurry you chime, we can't be late,
It's 10 minutes until they close the gate,
Get your shoes on, you gently call,
Because you don't want to raise your voice or get angry at all,
Call them to the front door,
But the shoes are still lying on the floor,
Put on your shoes you say in a high-pitched moan,
As the children move slowly and let out a groan,
Get all the things into the car in a hurry,
We will be the gate, don't you worry,

Return to the house to gather the kids,
What part of put on your shoes did they miss?
Put on your shoes, you say, louder than before,
No need to shout, they implore!
Finally, we are in the car and on our way,
Mummy, you hear,
Did you know it's a dress-up day!

One Day

One day you will be grown,
And these moments in time will have flown,
So, despite the work there is to do
I'm going to sit here and cuddle you,
It's not easy being a single mummy,
But while you are snuggled on my tummy,
I can't help feeling so very blessed,
So, I'll enjoy this cuddle and ignore the mess!!

Five Minutes Peace

Oh, how I long for five minutes of peace,

Just to breathe,

Or even go for a pee!

But as I try and as I rest,

I don't get five minutes alone,

Not even to get dressed.

"Muuum!" they call with all their might,

From dawn's first glow to late at night.

One needs toast cut corner to corner,

The others lost their shoes *again* this morning.

The bathroom's never truly mine,

There's banging, shouting - every time!

A sock emergency, a sibling war,

A knock, a cry, a slammed shut door.

I hide in the bathroom to clear my head,

Or pretend I'm busy to take a few minutes' rest.

I scroll my phone upon the loo,

But someone's always needing you

Yet in the chaos, in the mess,

Amongst the noise and lack of rest,

I wouldn't trade this kind of wild

For silence, if it meant no child.

Still… just once, I might just plea,
For a solo bath or a wee in peace, maybe?

Chapter Eleven
The Weight of It All

Carrying my work forward - this passion, this purpose - comes with a weight. A beautiful weight, yes, but a heavy one all the same.

When you're a professional in SEND and come from a place of lived experience, the lines between personal and professional blur quickly. Every child I support reminds me of my own. Every battle I fight echoes those I've fought around my own kitchen table. There is no off switch. No tidy separation. I carry it all - always.

And I carry it alone.

Being a single mother to neurodivergent children, while working, studying, and trying to carve out a career in a system not built for people like me - it's exhausting. Some days I feel like I'm running on fumes, barely holding the pieces together. I'll work all day, write essays through the night, comfort meltdowns at 3 a.m., and still try to show up with a smile in the morning. The pressure to be everything, to never drop the ball, can be suffocating.

There are moments I question everything.

Am I doing enough for my children?
Am I doing enough for myself?
Am I allowed to slow down - to rest?
Who supports the supporter?

And then there's the mask.

The one I wear in meetings. The one I wear to appear competent, articulate, "together." The one I learned to wear long before I even knew I was masking. Because I've had to. Because neurodivergent women are so often expected to perform at a level that denies their own needs - just to be taken seriously.

The truth? I don't always have it together. I burn out. I freeze. I cry behind closed doors. I question my worth. I grieve the quiet moments I've missed while holding everything else up.

But here's the other truth: I get back up. Every time.

Not just because I have to. Not only because others depend on me. But because I *want* to. Because I *believe* in this work. Because even when it feels impossible, I know I'm making a difference. For my children. For other families.

For the version of me who once felt voiceless, overwhelmed, and unseen.

Balancing it all is messy. It's imperfect. It's deeply human.

But if there's one thing I know now, it's this: I may carry a lot - but I carry it with purpose.

Burnout and Recovery

Burnout, for me, doesn't come with warning signs. It doesn't ask politely. It arrives like a sudden collapse after months of sprinting on uneven ground.

One minute I'm powering through, writing, advocating, fixing things, holding space for everyone around me, and the next, I'm barely able to function. I find myself staring at the same page for hours, forgetting appointments, snapping at people I love, crying for reasons I can't name. I stop answering messages. Stop showing up. Stop recognising myself.

This is what ADHD burnout looks like, especially for women who are constantly in survival mode. And when you layer on trauma, neurodivergence, single parenthood, professional pressure, and a lifetime of masking, it becomes more than just exhaustion. It becomes depletion. Like your nervous system has been scraped raw.

The world doesn't always see it, though. Because I'm "high-functioning" (A phrase I do not like) Because I smile. Because I keep going until I physically can't. Burnout in neurodivergent women is often misdiagnosed as depression or anxiety, when in fact, it's the natural consequence of living in a world that constantly demands more than we have to give (Raymaker et al., 2020).

And the recovery? It's slow. It's nonlinear. It isn't fixed with a bubble bath or a day off. Recovery means permitting myself to stop performing. It means lowering the bar, even when I feel guilty. It means cancelling plans, saying no, letting go of perfection. It means reconnecting to what soothes me - writing, rest, silence, the safety of being alone in my thoughts without trying to solve everything.

Sometimes recovery is ugly. It's lying in bed while dishes pile up. It's not answering the phone. It's sitting in the discomfort of stillness when your brain wants to run. But in those moments, I've started to learn how to be kinder to myself. I'm unlearning the belief that my worth is tied to my productivity.

I'm beginning to understand that burnout isn't a personal failure, it's a signal. It's my body saying, *enough. You matter, too.* And if I truly want to keep showing up, for my children, for my work, for the world, I have to show up for myself first.

Recovery isn't always graceful. But it's necessary. And every time I burn out, I rise a little slower, a little softer, and a little wiser than before.

I've been to the bottom

I've been to the bottom, and I've stared in the eyes of deathly fear,
And although I've not ended it in those moments of dread,
I have been very near,
But every time I visit that place of despair,
and overwhelming electricity runs through my veins,
I know it's not where I belong and that I will rise again,
For my journey is not destined to end in that way,
I'm here to see it through, to do hard things,
I'm here to stay.
I've got big plans, dreams and goals,
And it won't be wasted when someone hurts my soul,
The anger and frustration I feel,
Will be put into my hustle and made into something real,
I won't sit back and be defeated by depression and sadness
I will win the battle and rise again as a badass,
A strong mother, a dreamer and an ambitious lady,
I won't let depression into what it wants to make me,
I'll fight the hard fight, I'll put in the work and the time,
To rise from the darkness again and achieve what I know is mine,
I'm an independent woman, I don't need a man,

And if anyone can go it alone, I know that I can,
I've achieved so much just being alone on my journey,
So, it's time to rise and let nothing deter me.

Rest if you must

Rest if you must, but do not quit,
The flame still flickers, it's just not fully lit.
You're not broken, just worn thin,
It's not the end; it's time to begin… again.

Your work's not done, though your shoulders ache,
You've given your all, for everyone's sake.
But strength is not in endless fight,
It's in knowing when to dim the light.

When burnout clouds your sky with grey,
And every step feels miles away,
Know this weight is not defeat,
It's your body begging you to take a seat.

Not all silence is sadness near,
Sometimes it's healing overcoming fear,
What feels like sorrow deep and wide,
May just be rest you've been denied.

So, pause.
Let stillness be your sacred art,

Not giving up just a restart.
Put down the load, breathe in the grace,
Let self-kindness take its place.

Then, rise,
Not because you must prove,
But because you've found your unique groove.
Rest if you must, but do not quit,
Your soul has more fire, this is not it.

Chapter Twelve
How Tinder became my emotional growth app

As I mentioned earlier in this book, I was single for five years. In that time, I've dated on and off, mostly through the modern gateway of digital romance: Tinder. My relationship with the app was as unstable as some of the men I matched with. I'd download it, delete it, re-download it after a glass of wine or on a lonely Friday night… and every time, much to my dismay, I was met with the same outcome: disappointment.

Some dates were forgettable. Others were amusing, awkward, or fleetingly promising. And then there are the ones that stand out - not because they led to love, but because they revealed something much more important: Truths about myself.

One date in particular sticks with me. I'd matched with someone who, from their pictures, seemed kind, interesting, and reasonably attractive. But when we met in person, I was met with a completely different man, one whose appearance, energy, and presence bore little resemblance to his online self. I'd been catfished. I should have walked away. I should have said, "This isn't okay," and honoured the boundary that was crossed. But instead, I sat with him. I listened. And, in true Kayleigh fashion, I offered a makeshift therapy session.

I listened to his story. He was clearly going through something heavy; his mental health was fragile, his confidence low. I found myself wanting to help him understand why he didn't feel safe being his true self, to encourage him to be comfortable in his own skin. I didn't realise it then, but that moment reflected an ingrained pattern I've come to recognise in myself: a mix of deep empathy, co-dependency, and ADHD-fuelled impulsivity.

Therapists and ADHD relationship experts echo what I've experienced: without structured communication, self-care, and firm boundaries, ADHD can fuel a cycle of over-giving and emotional burnout (Riviera Therapy, 2024; Inclusive Teach, 2024). Research shows that emotional dysregulation is a common- but under-recognised -symptom of adult ADHD (Wikipedia, 2025). When paired with codependent tendencies - the urge to rescue, to hold boundaries loosely - it becomes a potent mix.

I didn't just stay for the drink. I gave him a lift home. He was anxious about getting the train, and I couldn't stand the thought of him being overwhelmed or panicking. Again, I poured from my own empty cup.

Because here's the thing: my time is like gold dust. I juggle motherhood, work, my own healing, and barely have time to breathe. Every moment I give to someone is precious. And yet, I gave that evening - my energy, empathy, petrol money - to a man who lied to me before we even met.

Women with ADHD are particularly vulnerable to entering unstable or imbalanced relationships due to emotional impulsivity, low self-esteem, and rejection sensitivity (Verywell Mind, 2024). My story - sitting through a catfish date, giving lifts to strangers, or staying with someone my intuition warned me about - is echoed across countless personal accounts and therapeutic case studies.

Do I still download Tinder now and then, usually after a glass of wine? Yes. Do I sometimes convince myself that this time will be different? Also yes. But I'm learning. Now, I ask different questions. Am I being loved, or am I being drained?

Am I being respected, or am I just being patient with red flags? Is this person filling my cup - or simply drinking from it?

Dating hasn't brought me the fairytale. But it's brought me back to myself. And that's a love story I'll never swipe left

Tinder

Few glasses of wine, download the app, hoping for something more,
Even though you've not found love there before,
Mindlessly swiping through all the men,
Only to be greeted with the same again,
Chris 40 stands proudly with his fish,
Finding a hookup is his only wish,
Here's Ben, married but he can explain,
That's why his profile pic is left plain,
How about Josh just here for some fun,
Why is it always the best-looking ones,
Another whose bio shows he's been hurt before
Only match if you chat is anyone genuine anymore,
George says his here for the long term but open to short,
Honestly, do these guys give this any thought?
Finally, find a match and await a reply,
Nice boobs he sends,
Oh my god, these men make me sigh,
Another match and he seems nice,
Just a shame he still lives with his ex-wife.
Get chatting to someone, and it's all going well,
He tells jokes and likes poetry as well,
Seems it's going better than most,

But before you know it, he turns into a ghost,
So, I'll delete it again for the 100th time,
Well, until I've had a few glasses of wine.

Chapter Thirteen
Negative Relationships

The Illusion of Love

This chapter is written from memory and emotion - my experience, as I lived and felt it.
It is not a statement of fact, but a reflection of how events impacted me personally.
Names and details may be changed or blended to protect identities.
This is not a mirror - it is a window into my truth.

Negative relationships have followed me throughout my life. I believe this is, in part, the legacy of my childhood trauma - of growing up with low self-esteem, of not knowing my worth, of being starved of emotional safety and taught to seek it outside myself. But I've come to understand there's more to it. My ADHD also plays a significant role. Women with ADHD are particularly vulnerable to toxic and abusive relationships, often due to impulsivity, emotional dysregulation, difficulty with boundaries, and an intense fear of rejection. Research suggests that women with ADHD are more likely to experience relational trauma and exploitation, in part because they crave deep connection and often doubt their own intuition.

I have lived this truth.

The first relationship I fell into following being single for five years, was with someone I met on tinder. In the beginning, I tried to tell myself it was real. I wanted so badly for it to be the fairytale, the happy ending I'd imagined in my head. For a while, it played the part. We went on city breaks, took photos that looked like love, did the things couples do. On the surface, it ticked the boxes.

But deep down, I knew something wasn't right. And I ignored it.

I had this nagging feeling that he wasn't over his ex-wife - or worse, that he was still with her in some way. There were little things, comments and inconsistencies, that whispered to me in the quiet moments. But I hushed them, choosing hope over reality. I didn't want another failed attempt. I didn't want to admit that once again, I'd trusted the wrong person. Then one night, the cracks turned into a fracture.

He got angry. Swearing and defensive. And just like that, I was no longer a woman in a relationship - I was a little girl again, back in a house where shouting and drinking went hand-in-hand. My nervous system didn't understand time. It just knew danger. The next part felt familiar, too: the lies. I found out he'd told me he was home, but in reality, he was at his ex-wife's house. My intuition hadn't been wrong - it had been right all along. I just didn't want it to be. So, I ended it. Quietly. Firmly. Because there wasn't anything left to fight for. Because love built on lies isn't love at all.

There isn't much more to say about him. He doesn't deserve much space in this book, or in my mind. But what he did prove, once again, is that men let me down. That trust is not something I hand over lightly anymore. That sometimes, love is just another mask someone wears to keep you from seeing who they really are. But more importantly, he reminded me of something else: That my intuition is not paranoid. It's not overreactive. It's my protector.

But nothing could have prepared me for what came next. It came from someone I should have been able to trust. Someone who shared my passion for inclusive education. Someone I had looked up to for the 18 months I'd known him. He was charming - not just with me, but with everyone. He had a protective energy, or at least he presented that way. He'd often say he "had my back."

One night, we were out just as friends, and he watched me. A few men approached me, and I saw something shift in his expression. Was it jealousy? Was it protectiveness? I wasn't sure. But he kept checking in on me, asking if I was okay. At one point, he took my hand, as if it were the most natural thing in the world. I remember thinking how right it felt. On the train home, he placed his hand on my thigh, and when we got off the train, he told me he couldn't look at me, or he'd kiss me. And he did. That kiss felt like the beginning of everything. The next time I saw him, he pushed me up against a wall and kissed me with the kind of urgency you only see in films - as if he'd been starved for that moment.

For the first month, he love-bombed me. He told me how special I was. How he couldn't stop thinking about me. How our connection was undeniable. He told me I had all of his attention. It was intoxicating - a rush of dopamine my ADHD brain clung to with both hands. For the first time, I thought, *This must be what love feels like.*

And I fell. I fell hard.

It wasn't the physical connection that held me; that part was never the hook. It was more. It was emotional. The pull that slips in unnoticed, settles deep in your chest, and whispers that it's love. What we had, or what I believed we had, went deeper than anything I'd known. The emotional intimacy, the passion, the way he made me feel like I was the only person in the world... It felt like a soul connection. Like something rare. Like something I had waited my whole life for.

Maybe it was our shared passions. Maybe it was trauma. Maybe it was my inner child, finally believing she had found safety in a man's arms. Or maybe it was ADHD - the way we feel everything tenfold, the way we romanticise intensity and mistake it for depth. The way we chase dopamine and ignore red flags is because we want to believe in love so badly.

There was one day I'll never forget. We held each other and kissed, and it was like lightning through my body. It wasn't just physical; it was soul-level. I let myself believe: *This is it. This is real.*

He even sent me poetry. No one had ever done that before. He knew how much I loved poetry, and he used it. I remember reading the first poem he sent, thinking, *I must be special. This must be real.* I believed he'd written it for me, about me, from a place of genuine affection.

But it was all part of the performance. He knew exactly how to reach me. He spoke to the deepest parts of me and drew me in with every word. Poetry was his key, and I was an open door.

Then things started to change. After a month of intense connection, he began pulling away. He'd say I was too good for him. That I deserved better. He told me he was broken, complex but couldn't let me go. He didn't want to see me with someone else. He said he couldn't bear it. And so, the push and pull began.

He messaged me almost every day for months. Every time we were alone, we were intimate, and he would reassure me time and time again that I was special, that he saw me in his life forever. He said his feelings for me were more than just physical. He even said I should see it as a compliment that he saw me as more than sex. Jeez, as I write this, I can't believe I didn't see those red flags being waved so obviously in my face. Everyone who cared for me warned me, they saw what he was doing, how my mental health was suffering.

He kept me close. But never publicly. Never in the light. I was a secret. A distraction. A moment.

…And then after six months, the truth came out: he had been in a relationship with someone else the entire time, someone he swore he wasn't with. His charm, his character, and his mask were all a show. He wasn't the person I thought he was - he was a manipulator. Everything he'd told me, everything he made me feel - all a lie. Everyone who had warned me was right.

The devastation was unlike anything I've ever felt. It wasn't just heartbreak. It was grief. Soul-shattering grief. Because I hadn't just lost him - I had lost the version of myself I believed was finally loved. I had believed in something real. I had opened myself up in a way I never had before. And it turned out, I was just a story he had written for his own gratification. He saw my vulnerabilities, and I was his prey. It impacted me in more ways than this, which I will not share here, just know that it was to be some of the hardest 12months of my life from the moment he took my hand that day.

How do you grieve someone who never truly existed, except in the illusion they sold you?

I'm still learning how.

What made it even harder was the timing. I found out just before Christmas. A time that should have been magical - all twinkling lights and warm traditions - instead became a surreal blur. I couldn't sleep. I couldn't eat. I felt numb on the inside. But I had to carry on. I had to keep the magic alive for my children. I had to smile, wrap presents, and sing songs, all while my soul felt like it was breaking apart.

I masked my way through it - because that's what I've always done. I've learned how to survive pain in silence. But inside, I was screaming.

Even now, months later, I'm still processing it all. The betrayal, the loss, the disorientation. There were moments I didn't want to be here anymore. I reached the bottom - the kind of darkness that wraps itself around your chest and whispers lies. But somehow, even in that pain, I held on.

Because of them.

My children have always been my lifeline. Just as I fiercely protect them, they unknowingly protect me. They are my reason. My anchor. My reminder that even when the world feels like it's crumbling, there is still light.

It's strange, really - how someone who entered my life for such a short time could leave such lasting damage. But I think that's the clearest sign of coercive control - of emotional manipulation. It doesn't need years. It just needs access. It just needs trust. And once it finds that crack in your defences, it slips in and rewires how you see yourself.

What I later came to understand is that what I had experienced was a form of *trauma bonding* - a psychological response to intermittent reinforcement and emotional abuse. When someone cycles between love and devaluation, it creates a powerful chemical addiction, especially for people who feel deeply or have a history of relational trauma. The very person who causes the pain becomes the only one who can soothe it, and so the cycle continues (Carnes, 2017). In many ways, it mimicked addiction - I craved his validation while being destroyed by his absence.

He rocked my core. Shook my sense of identity. The woman I had carefully rebuilt through motherhood, through education, through healing, suddenly felt unstable again. But she's still here. And maybe, despite it all, that's a victory.

These next poems reflect the arc of that story (there are quite a few, because poetry was - and is - how I process big feelings): from the high of believing I was loved, to the depths of realising I was only ever used.
But I survived. I'm still here. And I'm learning that love, when it comes, should feel like peace, not confusion. That passion without respect is not love. And that I, too, am worthy of a love that is honest, whole, and real.

My soul

He touches my soul in a way like never before,
And with each fleeting moment we share together it makes me want him more and more,
The connection that's felt is not something earthly bound,
It's a magnetic energy that within the universe can be found,
But only when two likened souls come together,
It's a question of will this last for ever?
But this feeling is addictive, like a sweet drug upon my lips.
I'm trying not to take too much and just have gentle sips,
Fear rushes through me in case I take too much,
And get lost within the lust, the electricity and the touch.

They spent the night together,

They spent the night together,
One that had been built on anticipation, excitement and lust,
They'd confided in each other even though they both find it hard to trust,
They wanted to escape the reality of their lives,
Away from their home town and prying eyes,
But it wasn't just passion that they found in each other,
Not just hot sex or a no strings attached lover,
Something deeper hit their souls that night,
As they stared into each other's eyes it just felt right,
But sex was not the hottest moment that night,
It was being close together; they felt the connection.
Rested on his chest, pulled close, held safe and no need for erection.

Fraud

She feels like a fraud as she can't see what he sees,
But she longs to relax, be herself and carefree,
She's insecure about her body and curves,
Even though she knows they don't define her worth,
She's scared if she fully lets down her mask and her walls,
That he won't be there and won't want to stay at all,
But each time she's with him, she's more her true being
And he reassures her that he likes what he is seeing,
A bond between them that's not easily explained,
But it's shared in their passions, their past and their pain,
There are fears around loyalty on both sides and worries about trust
As at the time they came together through their uncontrollable lust,
But he says that she's safe and she feels it in his actions,
And I hope he knows that she's loyal from her reactions,
In time they will get there and both feel secure,
As they continue to fall deeper and trust a bit more,
The passion that burns is hotter than any they've felt in the past,
And so, they both hope they've found something that will last

Are you thinking about me too

Are you thinking about me too?
When my brain won't let me forget about you?
Do I appear in your mind throughout the day?
Are you reminded of me by the things people say?
Do you see things and hear lyrics that spark a memory?
Do you think about me even though we were temporary?
Do you think about me too?
Because my brain won't let me stop thinking about you.

Twin flames

I feel I've known you all my life
And when you speak, my mind knows what you will say,
The energy around us feels the same as electricity on the same frequency,
And although I'm not with you all the time I feel you every day,
I can tell when you're sad, hurting or scared,
I know how you pretend not to care,
And we might fight it and try to push away,
But that energy I think, will always stay.
A twin flame, maybe or a similar soul,
Those feelings they like to take control,
Tell me I'm wrong, you don't feel the same,
That you don't feel that energy even at the mention of my name.
Your arms feel like home when you hold me so tight,
How can something be wrong when it feels so right…

Unspoken

I try to explain what I mean in words,
But it doesn't come out how I want to be heard.
So maybe I'll put it into a poem,
And hope it's easier for you to know then.
Not sharing our love with the world outside,
Makes me wonder what you're trying to hide.
And as much as I want to trust what you say,
My overthinking gets in the way.
I'm not asking for grand displays or fame,
Just not to feel like I'm playing a game.
I'm asking you to shift your pattern,
But it's starting to feel like I don't matter.
I don't want to beg, or plead, or chase,
I just want to know I have a place.
Somewhere secure, not left in doubt,
A love that's proud to be spoken about.
So, if I seem distant, quiet, or cold,
Know it's not anger, its fear taking hold.
I just want to feel seen, not hidden away -
Is that too much to ask of love today?

Weighted blanket

It's like the world just melted away,
When his arms wrapped around me like a weighted blanket,
That meant more than any whimsical words he could say,

Every burden and heartache were gone like a settled storm,
On a day that had seen torrential rain,
This embrace was like no other it exceeded the norm.
But it meant nothing to him at that time,
The feelings he had were clever actors,
His feelings were not the same as mine,
I felt it, though, like electricity through my veins,
He spoke words like he felt it too
But now a broken circuit is all that remains,
But how I long to feel that feeling again,
Even though it feels like I've been cut with a knife,
And that I'll be eternally sworn off men,
I don't want to be a fool brought down to the level of a clown,
I'm not in that circus,
And so, I'll rise above, I will not drown.

I guess that's not me

He said he usually gets what he wants,
So I guess that's not me,
He's pulled away, can't quite end it fully
But when I look in his eyes,
It's not the same spark I see,
Instead, there's sadness, confusion and hurt,
As he tries to decide if it could work,
At least that's what he told me,
He's weighing up the pros and cons,
Worried more now that it may go wrong,
But I'm not here to wait for my fate to be made up,
I'm worth more,
I'm worth romance and true love,
And although I know that's something
That could come in time,
I want someone who looks at me and thinks,
That girl, that girl, she's mine,
No second-guessing,
no doubts or being swayed by
outsiders' views,
Instead, someone who to his word is true,
I just want to know where I stand,
And if he regrets ever holding my hand

She's lost and she's not being found

She's lost and she's not being found,
It's not clear to her who she needs or wants to be around,
Perhaps being alone is where it is safe,
Away from all people and in her own space,
But she doesn't get much time for that, people demand her attention, and they want her back,
There's no time to ground those thoughts that rush through her mind like a train too fast for its track,
She's made her decisions,
And I guess there is no going back from that.
Being alone is something she knows best
because having that time to truly invest,
in somebody who might not give her what she needs,
Perhaps she just needs to be completely free
She's got so much love to give, though,
So much within her touch,
But she's lost,
And she doesn't know who deserves her that much,
She's tired,
She's tired from constantly overthinking her relationships,
Perhaps that have all sunk now though like a broken ship,
She's trying to keep her head afloat,

and not sink below the surface where she knows it's dark

and there is no hope,

She's been there before, and she survived,

But maybe if she goes there again.

She won't come out alive.

The nice guy disguise

The nice guy disguise doesn't wash with me no more,
When I looked into those eyes,
I was a fool for what I thought I saw,
Not ambition, not sparkle, but more a dark secret,
And you pulled me in, expecting me to keep it,
You say you're not good with words,
But I guess that's just an excuse,
So that when you say something mean to me,
It's a reason you can use,
You pulled me in love bombing from the very start,
And then when you thought that you'd got my heart,
You just offered out breadcrumbs to keep me coming back,
And although you said it was complicated, i
t was the truth that you lacked,
The perfect situationship getting what you need,
While all you offered me was breadcrumbs and some seeds,
And when I tried to pull away and focus on myself again,
You said that you cared for me, I was special and more
than just friends,
Then the truth is revealed, and I don't know you at all,
Again, I feel embarrassed for being such a fool,
You took my respect and wrecked it with your greed,

You used my good nature to gratify your needs,
You've lied to so many people and crushed so many hearts,
All I wish is that I'd have seen it right from the start,
I value honesty, I value directness and truth,
But none of those things have I ever got from you.

They thought I was weak

They thought I was weak,
That I'd just bow down,
Take in the water they kept pouring
And drown,
They underestimated me,
They don't know me that well after all,
They thought I'd crumble, they thought I'd fall,
But here I stand stronger than before,
Not fooled by their falsities anymore,
I will not stand by and be defeated,
Despite the actions, so conceited,
My journey continues to rise above,
Surrounded by people that I love,
Success in everything that I've done,
So go ahead, underestimate me,
That will be fun.

A shadow of who she was

And there she stood a shadow of who she was,
Affected by heartache, trauma and loss,
But here she cannot stay nor wallow,
Even though her heart bleeds and her veins are hollow,
She must pick up the pieces shattered in the storm,
To re-light the fire that burned before her hopes were torn,
Remembering who she was before she was greeted by pain,
To try to move forward now and forget his name,
All of her being aches from the journey she endured,
At the hands of a person who she has now mourned,
His death didn't happen for he was never alive,
His personality built on charm, falsities and lies,
Words cannot describe what it feels like to miss a person whose mortal life did not exist,
For the person of fabrication was all that she missed,
She has to come to terms with the lies that were told,
And see the truth for what it was and allow the reality to unfold,
This queen cannot be beaten,
This is not a defeat,
She will rise from the shadows, she will learn from the deceit,

Once again, her spark will return,

The fire will burn,

She will be free of pain, her eyes now opened wide,

The pieces back together, and now she rides the turning

tide

The Things I Want to Say

The Things I Want to Say
I can forgive, but I won't forget,
Giving you access to me
Was my deepest regret.
You held the key to a sacred space,
And turned it cold,
Such a warm-hearted place.

You didn't deserve to know me that well,
To sit in my silence,
To hear what I'd tell.
You wore masks with ease,
Always hiding to stop me seeing,
Laced in deception,
Poisoned my being.

You lied with a tongue dipped in sugar and smoke,
Each word you spoke
Was another cruel joke.
Your love came in riddles,
In games and in tricks,
You played with my heart

Just to get your fix.

But I'm not the girl you thought I would be,
I saw through your shade,
Now I walk free.
You mistook kindness for weakness,
Mistook silence for shame,
But I've risen from ruins,
Stronger, untamed.

You don't get the poems,
The parts of my soul,
You chipped at my edges,
But I've filled every hole.
And maybe I'm softer,
But I'm wiser too,
I learned that betrayal
Can come dressed like you.

I won't wish you harm,
I won't scream or fight,
But I'll write what you did
In the pages of night.
And when peace finds me,

It won't ask your name,
Because healing looks nothing
Like playing your game.

So, here's to the truth
You tried to erase,
I've found my power
In every place.
I forgive, but I don't forget,
And that's as close to mercy
As you'll ever get.

I fell for you

I fell for you,

The charm, the passions, the dream,

But nothing was quite what it seemed,

You fed me lies so easily,

Rose-tinted my glasses so I could not see,

Your true intention is to manipulate and coerce,

I've felt pain before, but this was far worse,

All of the trauma came rushing through,

Every pain resurfaced because of you,

Every man in my life has let me down,

And I entered your circus, you treated me like a clown,

But I will not dance amongst fools like you,

You don't deserve to be part of this book.

But you're part of my story, for I mistook,

Manipulation for love and care,

Lies convinced me you'd always be there,

Oh, what a fool I was to trust you,

For you to trample my heart because that's what you do,

You pick your prey and play your game,

And you treat people who love you all the same,

I was a mouse, and you were the cat,

I didn't deserve to be treated like that.

She knows

She knows it's time to let go and time for change,
As the end of the year becomes close in range,
She knows 2025 is for a fresh start to explore new places,
As she prepares to start something fresh and meet new faces,
She knows she'll meet people within her league,
That won't lie, cheat or try to deceive,
She knows it's about to get a lot better, and she will shine,
Because this last chapter is only a moment in time.
She knows.

Chapter Fourteen
Rising Again

How I Overcame

I've overcome so much on this journey, more than I sometimes give myself credit for. And along the way, I've learned to become kinder to myself. To stop seeing my struggles as personal failings, and instead to see them as part of the beautiful, complicated way my neurodivergent brain works.

Positive affirmations and mindfulness have played such an important role in helping me manage the parts of ADHD that felt overwhelming, especially growing up. I remember my mum reading *Feel the Fear and Do It Anyway*. She filled our home with positive affirmations, plastered them on the walls, the mirrors, and looking back, I believe they had a profound impact on me.

Through my study of psychology, I've come to understand just how powerful our self-talk is. The things we tell ourselves shape our reality. We don't always see that our mindset, positive or negative, becomes the lens through which we experience the world. If we wake each day and tell ourselves, *Today is going to be a good day. Everything is well in my world*, we are setting the stage for positivity. But if we start the day expecting struggle, expecting failure, that too can become our truth.

This isn't just wishful thinking or pseudoscience; it's backed by research. Positive affirmations change the way our brain works. They help us rewire our thoughts. Some of the affirmations I repeat most often are:

I am a positive, self-assured, and confident person.

Everything I touch is a success.

My mind is relaxed. My body is relaxed.

The best time to practice these affirmations is at the quiet edges of the day, just before sleep and right when you wake. Those moments when the mind is open, when the words can sink in deepest.

Another tool that has helped me is therapy. People often assume that because I've studied psychology, I must have it all figured out. But here's the thing: knowing the theory doesn't mean I'm immune to the pain.

I can explain why trauma responses exist, name every stage of grief, identify a dozen cognitive distortions in a single conversation, and still find myself crying in the car park after holding it together all day.

I can tell someone else how to reframe their inner critic... and still crumble under the weight of mine.

Therapy taught me that healing isn't academic. It's not about ticking boxes or passing modules. Healing is messy, nonlinear, and often inconvenient. It shows up when you least expect it, in the way you flinch at kindness, or freeze when asked how *you're* doing.

Therapy helped me start to notice those moments. It helped me give them names, not just definitions. There's something sacred about therapy - about being in a room, or on a screen, where nothing is expected of you except honesty. No one needs their shoes found. No one needs a sandwich made. No one is judging your tone or waiting for you to be "fine." It's a space where I can say, "I'm not okay," and no one rushes to fix it - they just stay with me in it.

Sometimes I spend the session talking non-stop. Other times, I sit in silence for what feels like forever. And in that silence, I've met parts of myself I didn't even know were there - the scared child, the angry woman, the grieving mother, the exhausted carer. Therapy lets me see her. And slowly, it's teaching me to love her too.

One of the most healing parts of therapy has been naming the shame I carry - and letting go of the belief that it's mine to hold. Shame from childhood. Shame from motherhood. Shame from abusive relationships, from mistakes, from breakdowns, from simply being human in a world that doesn't always allow women like me to fall apart. Therapy didn't remove the past, but it loosened the grip it had on me. It gave me permission to ask, "What would I say to a friend in this situation?" And then to try - gently - to say it to myself.

Before therapy, I lived with a harsh inner voice. One that said: "You're too much." "You're not enough." "You should be over this by now." "You're failing." That voice didn't start with me. It was shaped by years of instability, abandonment, and being made to feel like I had to earn love. Therapy taught me that I could rewrite the script. That I could challenge that voice. That self-compassion isn't indulgent - it's essential. And now, when that voice returns, I have another one that gently replies: "She's doing her best. Let her breathe."

So many people say to me, "You're so strong." And yes - I am. But strength doesn't mean I don't struggle. Strength is showing up to therapy even when it hurts. It's saying, "I need help," when my instinct is to say, "I'm fine."

It's choosing healing, over and over again. I've built so much of my life on holding others - my children, the families I supported, friends, and strangers in need. But therapy reminded me: I deserve to be held too.

Therapy hasn't made life easier; it's made me stronger in the face of life's chaos. It's taught me that rest is a right, not a reward. That feeling doesn't make me weak. That I can be both healing and whole, a work-in-progress and worthy. It's the place I've learned to take off the mask and start living beyond it.

Therapy Taught Me

Therapy taught me to leave things behind,
That not every shadow needs space in my mind.
That wounds from the past don't define who I am,
And survival itself is a kind of "I can."

Therapy taught me I'm allowed to feel,
That healing is messy but beautifully real.
That crying isn't weakness, it's letting it go,
And sometimes the strongest just don't let it show.

Therapy taught me to speak my own name,
To stop shrinking myself in the face of shame.
To set firm boundaries, say what I mean,
To clean out the thoughts that were never that clean.

Therapy taught me to breathe and be still,
To stop racing forward, just chasing the will.
To sit with my pain, not run from the fight,
To find tiny moments of peace in the night.

Therapy taught me I'm more than the ache,
More than the trauma, the guilt, the mistake.

That I deserve love, even on days
I don't feel worthy in any way.

And most of all
Therapy taught me to stay.
To not walk away from myself anymore.
To open the wounds,
Then *heal* from the core

If I could leave you with one message, it's this: You *can* rise. You *will* rise. And when you do, you'll see that everything you thought made you weak was actually what made you strong.

Planting Seeds: My Spiritual Path

I wouldn't describe myself as extreme in my spirituality, but I've always felt connected to something bigger than myself. I've always been drawn to mindfulness, gratitude, and the idea that we are just a small part of a vast, incredible universe. There is so much more than just *us*, and I find peace in that.

I believe in the power of intention. In the power of planting seeds in our minds and nurturing them with action. I believe in living with purpose, setting goals with clarity, and trusting that we can achieve what we set out to do. Everything starts as a thought. Every invention, every creation on this earth began in the mind of someone who dared to imagine it.

As someone with ADHD, my mind is always creating. And in that, I see a gift, because we are more likely to become entrepreneurs, creatives, and visionaries. We have constant ideas flowing, and when we learn to focus those ideas with intention, incredible things can happen.

I've seen this in my own life. I believe I manifested my first-class degree. I visualised it, I felt what it would mean to achieve it, and then I put in the work. The same with my psychology master's degree. And now, I hold the vision of my next goal: to achieve a doctorate in educational psychology. I can already see it, feel it, as though it's mine, and I know I will work to make it so.

Even my home, the one I sit in as I write this, came from planting seeds of intention. I remember sitting in the garden of our small two-up two-down in a lovely village. I was grateful for that home, for the 14 years we'd spent there, for the memories, the four home births that took place within those walls. But with five children, I knew it was time for something more. I sat quietly, meditating, expressing gratitude and visualised our next home. A four-bedroom detached house. I pictured every part of it. I felt what it would be like to live there. And within weeks, I received a letter offering us exactly that an affordable rent home that matched the vision I had held.

For me, spirituality is about that blend of gratitude, intention, and action. It's about believing in possibility, picturing it, and working for it. Nothing is truly out of reach when you plant the seeds, nurture them, and trust in the journey.

Seeds of Intention

I plant my dreams like seeds in soil,
softly, quietly, with care.
I picture them,
the home, the work, the path,
as though they're already there.

My mind, a garden wild and full,
with thoughts that bloom and race.
A hundred ideas take root at once,
each reaching out for space.

I water them with gratitude,
with faith that's calm and true.
What starts as a thought becomes my world,
I build it. I see it through.

I've learned a lot about myself on this journey so far - and I know I'm not even halfway through my story. Life has tested me, shaped me, broken me open and stitched me back together in ways I never expected. But one thing I know for certain: we *can* learn, we *can* heal, and we *can* rise again.

The painful things that happen to us, the traumas, the losses, the betrayals - they leave their mark, yes. But they also carve out space inside us for strength, for empathy, for growth. I believe those experiences shape us into who we're meant to be.

I believe we each have a purpose in this life. Mine, I've come to see, is to help others - to stand beside those who are struggling, especially those navigating the world through the lens of neurodivergence. My purpose is to speak up, to advocate, to help create a world that doesn't just *tolerate* difference but celebrates it. A world where neurodivergent people don't have to mask, don't have to apologise for who they are, don't have to fight to be understood.

And I will continue to do that. In my work, in my words, in the way I raise my children and live my life.

I hope that in sharing this story - in these chapters and poems - I have offered you a sense of empowerment. A reminder that even in your hardest moments, you are not alone. That it is good to be different. That our brains, our ways of seeing and feeling the world, are gifts.

Without the diversity of our minds, this world would be a far duller, less vibrant place. So, let's honour that difference. Let's rise, together.

Wouldn't it be boring if we were all the same

Wouldn't it be boring if we were all the same?
Same looks, same likes and same brain?
Wouldn't it be bad to have limited thinking?
No creative thoughts or patterns linking,
Imagine a world without inventions and theory,
Wouldn't it all become a bit dreary?
Wouldn't it be bad if we didn't have passions?
For the environment, for nature and creative fashion,
Wouldn't it be bad without those powers?
To not be able to hyper-focus for hours,
Wouldn't it be bad not to have the success?
That comes when your brain doesn't work like the rest?
Imagine if we hadn't had Einstein, Darwin or Mozart,
And that's just a few famous names for a start,
Imagine no Van Gogh, Warhol, da Vinci or Burton,
Our world would be much more dull, I'm certain,
We need to embrace and accept all brains,
Because wouldn't it be boring we all thought the same?..

A Vision for the Future

My hope for the future is simple - and yet, revolutionary. I want a world where neurodivergent people are not only accepted, but *understood, celebrated,* and *empowered.*

Too often, ADHD and autism are painted with a single brush, oversimplified, misunderstood, or worse, pathologised beyond recognition. But neurodivergence is not black and white. It is not a checklist of traits or a character on TV. It is rich and layered. It is a spectrum, vast and complex. No two neurodivergent people are the same. Each brain is unique, wired in its own beautiful, brilliant way. I want the world to see this. To know this. Because **neurodivergent minds have always shaped the world** through art, through science, through activism and innovation. Without us, the world would be missing some of its most creative, intuitive, and justice-driven souls.

Yet we are too often told we must change to fit the systems around us. We are told we are too much, too sensitive, too distracted, too different. But the truth is - *it's the systems that need to change.*

I dream of a world where the education system, the workplace, and our social norms adapt to *us* - not the other way around. A world where children like mine grow up feeling safe in their bodies, confident in their differences, and free to be exactly who they are. Where they don't just survive in mainstream spaces - they thrive.

I hope my children, and all children like them, grow up in a society that *sees* them, truly sees and embraces them with compassion, not correction. A world that doesn't ask them to mask or shrink or bend themselves into painful shapes to belong.

I hope we replace shame with curiosity. Stigma with support. Silence with *story*.

And personally, I hope to continue this mission. I hope to earn my PhD in educational psychology. But more than that - I want to *do something with it.* I want to be part of real change. To work at the heart of education, inclusion, and reform. To speak out, write loudly, share my truth, and amplify the voices of others still finding theirs. To use my experience not as a scar, but as a tool for advocacy - for change.

This book is one step.

But I hope it becomes a doorway.

For more awareness. More compassion.

And more spaces where neurodivergent people are not made to feel *less than* -but *more than enough.*

A Future Rewritten

I dream of a world not built on compliance,
Where difference is met not with silence,
But song,
Where every mind, no matter its pace,
Has the freedom to find its own place.

A world where children aren't told to behave,
By dimming the fire that makes them brave.
Where stimming is dancing,
And fidgeting's grace,
Where no one is punished for needing their space.

I dream of classrooms with flexible light,
Sensory spaces and justice done right.
Not boxes and rows,
Not shame and reward,
But love as the structure,
And voice as the board.

I dream of systems that listen and bend,
Not force us to fracture or break just to mend.
Of stories like mine being bridges, not chains,
Of mothers with swords who carry the flames.

I want my children to grow in a land,
Where "different" means powerful, curious, grand.
Where no one must mask just to belong,
And quiet is valid, as well as the strong.

So, I write, and I speak, I advocate loud,
For the wild ones, the soft ones, the ones not yet proud.
We were never too much, we were never too wrong,
Just waiting for systems to catch up all along.

The ADHD Self Help Toolkit

Understanding yourself: Self-Discovery Tools

This toolkit is born from lived experience, not just theory. As a neurodivergent woman and mother, I know how easy it is to feel overwhelmed, misunderstood, or invisible - especially when juggling the demands of life, parenting, and navigating a world that often isn't built for minds like ours.

The tools included here are the ones that helped me survive, grow, and eventually thrive. They are a blend of psychological strategies, affirmations, prompts, and practical tips - all grounded in compassion and flexibility. You won't find rigid advice or one-size-fits-all rules. Instead, you'll find options. Gentle guidance. Space to reflect and reconnect with yourself.

You don't have to use everything. Some pages might resonate deeply; others might not feel relevant right now - and that's okay. Come back to them when you're ready. This is your space, your journey, your story.

Most of all, this toolkit is here to remind you:

- You are not broken.
- You are not alone.
- You are worthy of peace, clarity, and joy.

1. Reframing Failures: From Shame to Growth

Failure. It's a word that often comes with shame, disappointment, and self-doubt. But what if we looked at failure differently?

As neurodivergent individuals, we may have faced more "failures" or perceived failures than others, misunderstood at school, judged in social settings, labelled in ways that made us feel broken. But every so-called failure was not the end. It was a redirection. A lesson. A chance to rise.

What is Reframing?

Reframing is the practice of changing the way we *see* something in order to change the way we *experience it*. It doesn't mean denying what happened, but instead choosing to extract *meaning* and *growth* from the situation.

"I failed at this"	"This was a learning experience"
"I'm not good enough"	"I haven't mastered it yet"
"They rejected me"	"That space wasn't aligned for me"

| "I always mess things up" | "Every mistake is helping me to grow" |

Why It Matters (Especially for ADHDers)

People with ADHD often experience **rejection sensitivity**, **low self-esteem**, and **perfectionism**. That means failure can feel devastating, like a reflection of who we are, not just what happened. But reframing gives you *your power back*. It reminds you that you are more than your mistakes, and that your path is *allowed* to be messy.

Reframing Practice:

1. Write down a recent "failure."

What happened? How did it make you feel?

2. **Ask: What did I learn from this?**

Even if it's small, maybe you learned something about your boundaries, your values, or what *not* to do.

3. **Now reframe it in a sentence.**

Example: "I missed that deadline" - "That showed me I need better support in planning. I'm not lazy, I'm learning."

4. **Say it out loud.**

Let yourself *feel* the new story. Believe it.

Affirmations for Reframing

- *I grow through what I go through.*

- *I am allowed to make mistakes and still be worthy.*

- *My path is not linear, and that's okay.*

- *I am learning, evolving, and becoming every day.*

- *There is wisdom in every misstep.*

Remember: Reframing doesn't erase what happened. It rewrites your *relationship* with it. You don't need to carry the weight of failure when you can carry the lesson instead.

2. Late ADHD Diagnosis Checklist

Have you ever felt like something just didn't quite "click," despite your best efforts? This reflective checklist may help you identify signs of ADHD that were missed earlier in life - especially in girls and women.

Emotional & Mental Patterns

- ☐ Often described as "sensitive," "daydreamy," or "too emotional" as a child
- ☐ Experienced intense emotions, especially around rejection or criticism
- ☐ Frequently overwhelmed by everyday tasks, but couldn't explain why
- ☐ Periods of depression or anxiety, often after burnout
- ☐ Diagnosed with anxiety, depression, or bipolar disorder before ADHD was ever mentioned

Behaviour & Focus

- ☐ Regularly lose or misplace everyday items (keys, phone, bank card)

- ☐ Constantly start new projects but struggle to finish them
- ☐ Difficulty focusing on boring or repetitive tasks - but hyperfocus on passions
- ☐ Easily distracted by noises, thoughts, or surroundings
- ☐ Interrupting or talking too much in conversations without meaning to

Organisation & Daily Life
- ☐ Cupboards and drawers often left open; tasks half-finished
- ☐ Lists help... but often get lost
- ☐ Frequently running late despite best intentions
- ☐ Overwhelm with adulting - appointments, forms, cleaning, etc.
- ☐ Relying on adrenaline or deadlines to get things done

Relationships & Social Life
- ☐ People-pleasing tendencies or trouble setting healthy boundaries

- ☐ Felt like an outsider, even with friends - "on the edge" of social groups
- ☐ Often exhausted after social events, needing long recovery
- ☐ Difficulty interpreting social cues, often overthinking past conversations
- ☐ Strong gut feelings or intuition, but unsure when to trust them

Childhood Clues (Retrospective)
- ☐ Struggled with reading or writing but knew you weren't "unintelligent"
- ☐ Reports/comments like "needs to try harder," "easily distracted," or "daydreamer"
- ☐ Found school hard to cope with emotionally or socially, despite being bright
- ☐ Family often missed the signs because "you coped" or because neurodivergence was normalised

Positive Traits (Often Overlooked!)
- ☐ Creative, passionate, and full of ideas
- ☐ Highly empathetic with a strong sense of justice

- ☐ Introspective, deep thinker, and emotionally intelligent
- ☐ Often the go-to person for advice or support
- ☐ Resilient and resourceful, especially in chaos

Note:

This is not a diagnostic tool, but if many of these resonate with you, it may be worth seeking a professional ADHD assessment. You are not lazy, broken, or "too much" - you are wired differently, and that difference holds power

If you've resonated with the experiences shared in this book and found yourself ticking off many items on the checklist, the next pages may be especially helpful.

It includes a template letter you can take to your GP to request an ADHD assessment.

In the UK, NHS waiting lists for adult ADHD assessments can be long, but it's important to know that you have the right to choose your provider. Some services, such as *Psychiatry UK*, often have shorter waiting times via the *Right to Choose* pathway.

I know many people question whether pursuing a diagnosis is worthwhile. For me, it was life changing. Receiving a diagnosis gave me answers to questions I'd carried for years- it helped me understand why I've always felt different. Most importantly, it gave me permission to show myself compassion, and to begin reshaping the negative narratives I had internalised.

If you're considering this step, know that you're not alone. Take this letter with you, advocate for yourself, and trust that you deserve support.

To:
[GP's Name or "The GP"]
[Your GP Surgery Name]
[Address of Surgery]

Subject: Request for ADHD Assessment – Adult Referral

Dear [Doctor's Name],

I am writing to formally request a referral for an assessment for **Attention-Deficit/Hyperactivity Disorder (ADHD)** in adulthood.

Over the years, I have noticed persistent difficulties that are consistent with ADHD, which have significantly affected my day-to-day functioning and overall well-being. These include:

- Ongoing difficulties with concentration and sustaining attention
- Challenges with organisation, time management, and forgetfulness
- Impulsivity, including interrupting others or making decisions quickly without thinking them through
- Emotional dysregulation, including frequent overwhelm and mood swings
- Restlessness or an inability to relax, even when trying to unwind

These symptoms have been present since childhood but were not recognised or diagnosed at the time. I now understand that ADHD can often go unnoticed in childhood, particularly in [insert relevant context – e.g., "girls/women" or "those with predominantly inattentive presentations"].

The impact on my life has been significant. [You may wish to briefly outline any specific difficulties here, e.g., in education, work, relationships, or mental health.]

After researching and speaking with others, I believe an assessment would help me better understand myself and access any support or treatment I may need. I understand that the NHS pathway usually involves referral to a local community mental health team or a specialist ADHD service, and I would be grateful if we could begin that process.

I appreciate your time and support with this matter. Please let me know if you require any additional information or would like to discuss this further.

Kind regards,
[Your Full Name]
[Date of Birth]
[NHS Number, if know

3. **Rejection Sensitivity Support Plan**

"Navigating Emotional Storms with Awareness, Compassion and Tools"

Step 1: Understand the Trigger

Ask yourself:
- What happened that made me feel rejected?
- Was it **actual rejection**, or did I **perceive it** that way?
- Is there **evidence** this person dislikes me or that I've done something wrong?

Reminder: ADHD brains are wired to seek connection and approval. Your feelings are valid, even if they aren't always based in fact.

Step 2: Name the Emotion
- Label what you're feeling: *"I feel embarrassed... hurt... ashamed... anxious..."*
- Validating your emotion takes power away from it.

Thought Trap	Reframe Thought Example
"They hate me."	"Maybe they were distracted or tired."
"I ruined everything."	"Everyone makes awkward comments. I'm human."
"They must be annoyed at me."	"It's okay if someone has a feeling. I'm still worthy."
"I can't cope with this."	"I've felt like this before, and I got through it."

- Use this mantra:

"This is rejection sensitivity, not reality."

Step 3: Use a Rejection Reframe Toolkit

Step 4: Soothe Your Nervous System

Rejection sensitivity activates the **fight/flight** response. Ground yourself:

- Breathe in for 4, hold for 4, out for 6
- 5-4-3-2-1 Grounding Exercise (5 things you see, 4 you can touch…)
- Repeat affirmations:

"I am not my feelings."
"This will pass."
"I am still loveable and enough."

Step 5: Create a Self-Compassion Ritual

After an RS episode, give yourself what you need:
- Write a **"note to self"** from your calm mind to your overwhelmed one
- Put your hand on your heart and say:

"It's okay. You're safe. You're learning. You're healing."

- Do something comforting: a warm drink, bath, favourite playlist, sit in the garden

Step 6: Build a Rejection Journal

Keep track of:
- What triggered you
- How you felt
- What you *thought* was true
- What you *later learned* or could reframe

Over time, this builds pattern awareness and self-trust.

Optional Rejection Reset Mantras
- "Rejection doesn't mean I'm unlovable."
- "Even if someone doesn't like me, I still like me."
- "Not being chosen isn't the same as being worthless."
- "Sometimes, no response is not personal."

4. Affirmations for Healing & Empowerment

Daily Grounding Affirmations
- *"I am safe, I am calm, I am centred."*
- *"My brain is wired differently, and that is not a flaw - it's a gift."*

- *"I release the need to be perfect. I honour progress over perfection."*

Affirmations for Rejection Sensitivity
- *"I am not defined by how others perceive me."*
- *"Their response is not a reflection of my worth."*
- *"I can feel rejection without letting it break me."*
- *"Even when I feel unloved, I am still loveable."*

Affirmations for ADHD Self-Compassion ....

I am not
lazy –
I am learning
to work with
my rhythm.

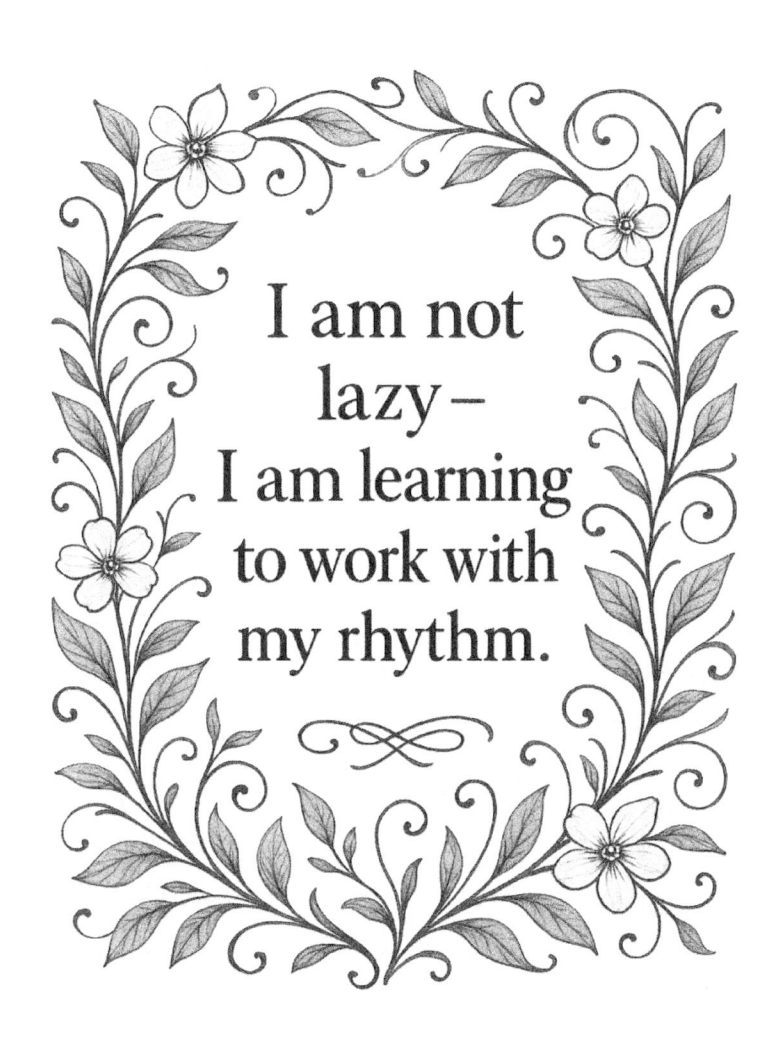

My
scattered
thoughts
hold
deep
wisdom

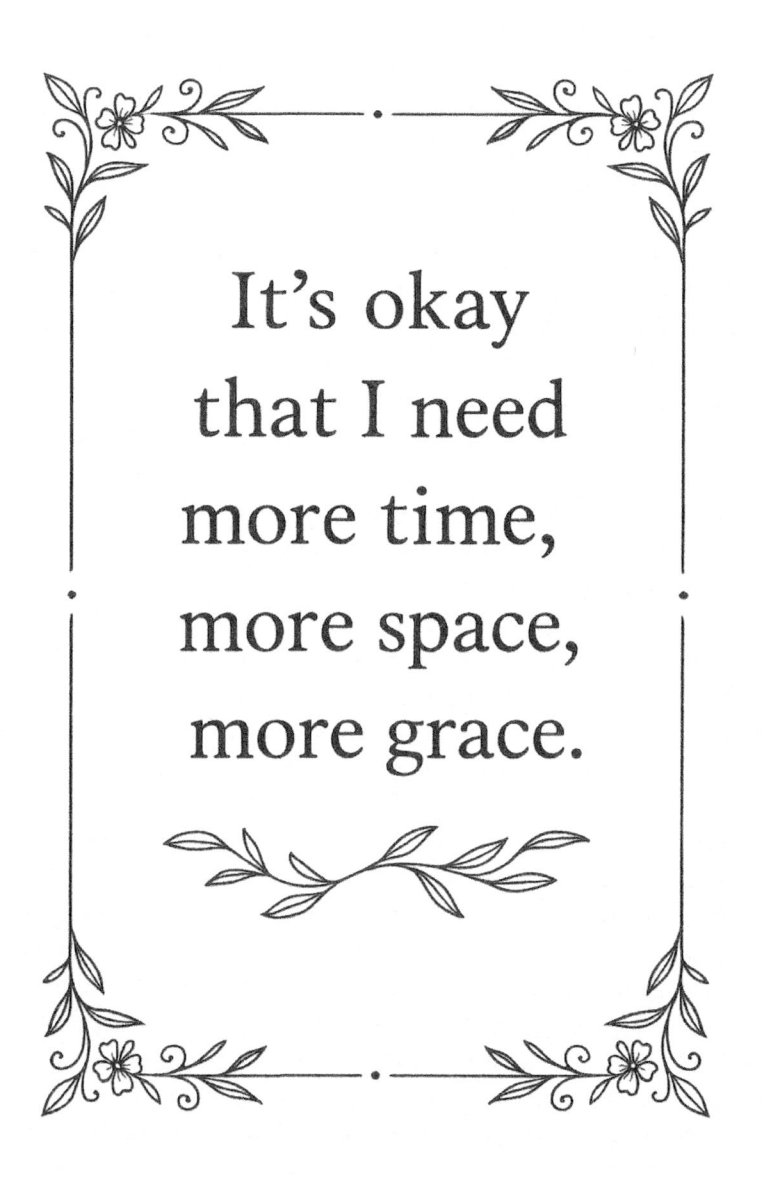

It's okay
that I need
more time,
more space,
more grace.

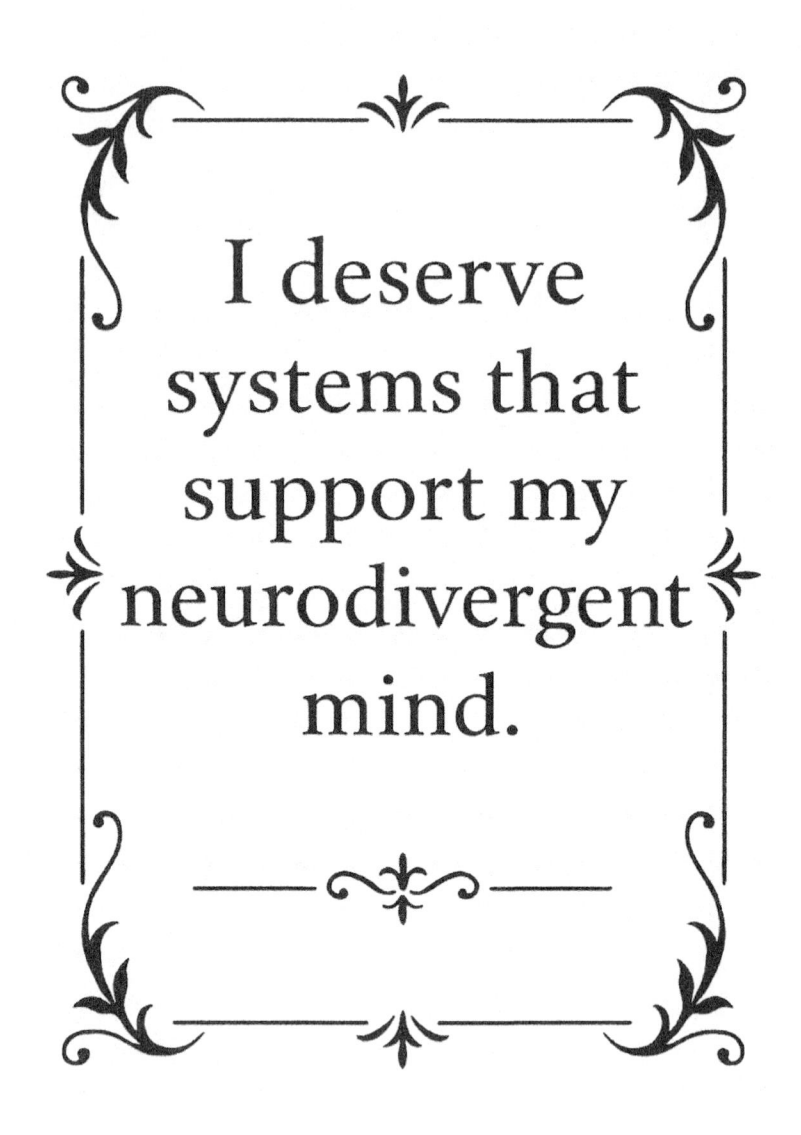

I deserve systems that support my neurodivergent mind.

Mantras for Boundaries & Self-Worth

- *"No is a full sentence."*

- *"I am allowed to walk away from what doesn't serve me."*

- *"I do not need to shrink myself to be accepted."*

- *"I am not here to be small; I am here to be real."*

Manifestation & Purpose

- *"Everything I need is already within me."*

- *"I am becoming the woman I once needed."*

- *"I trust the timing of my life."*

- *"Each step forward, no matter how small, is sacred."*

5. Life with ADHD: Practical Hacks

Living with ADHD can be beautifully chaotic - but with the right tools and mindset, you can make it work *for* you. Here are some practical hacks that can help you stay on top of everyday life while honouring the way your brain works:

Daily Routines & Structure
- Use visual schedules or planners (digital or paper) to keep track of the day.
- Break tasks into bite-sized chunks and use a timer (e.g., Pomodoro method: 25 minutes on, 5-minute break).
- Create morning and evening routines with clear steps (write them down or post them somewhere visible).

Reminders & Prompts

For ADHD brains, memory and time awareness can be inconsistent, especially when juggling multiple roles and tasks. It's not about laziness or forgetfulness -it's about how executive function works differently. That's why externalising memory through alarms, sticky notes, and visual cues is so important. These tools act as gentle nudges, bringing attention back to what matters before it slips through the cracks. Labelled alarms and visible prompts reduce mental load and decision fatigue, helping you move through your day with more ease, less stress, and greater self-compassion.

- Set multiple alarms and phone reminders with *labels* ("Pick up Daisy" not just "Alarm").
- Use sticky notes around the house for regular tasks (e.g., "Take meds" on the fridge).
- Place visual cues near exits: keys, bags, forms, etc.

Declutter Your Space

For many people with ADHD, "out of sight" often means "out of mind." This is due to challenges with object permanence - the ability to remember things that aren't directly in front of you. That's why visibility and accessibility are key. Clear containers, open shelves, and strategic storage help reduce frustration and increase functionality. But it's also important to keep expectations realistic. Aim for systems that work for *you*, not Pinterest-worthy perfection. "Organised chaos" can be a valid, effective approach. Store items where you naturally reach for them and simplify where you can. The goal is not tidiness for its own sake - but a space that reduces overwhelm and supports your unique rhythm.

- Keep everything visible - clear boxes, open shelving, and labels help with object permanence.
- Declutter often, but *realistically*- aim for "organised chaos" over perfection.
- Store things where you use them (e.g., scissors in the room you most often need them).

Focus Tools

Staying focused with ADHD isn't about trying harder - it's about working *with* your brain, not against it. Tools like brown noise, instrumental music, and binaural beats can help filter distractions and create a calming sound environment that supports concentration. Body doubling - working alongside someone else, even through a video call - can spark motivation and reduce procrastination. Likewise, fidget tools or chewable jewellery provide sensory input that helps regulate the nervous system, allowing the brain to stay present. These strategies aren't crutches - they're supports that honour how your mind functions best, helping you get into flow without the shame of forcing it.

- Listen to instrumental music, brown noise, or binaural beats while working.
- Try body doubling (working alongside someone else, even virtually).
- Use fidget tools or chewable jewellery to stay regulated while concentrating.

Energy Management

Managing energy is just as important as managing time -especially for those with ADHD. Neurodivergent energy often comes in waves, with bursts of motivation followed by deep fatigue. Trying to force productivity during low-energy periods can lead to burnout, frustration, and shame. Instead, honour your natural rhythm. Use your high-energy windows for tasks that require more focus or decision-making and give yourself permission to rest *before* you're running on empty. Planning for rest isn't indulgent - it's essential. When you build your life around energy awareness rather than rigid schedules, you create a more sustainable, self-compassionate way of being.

- Honour your natural energy flows - don't force productivity during burnout.
- Use "high energy" moments for admin and decision-making.
- Build in rest time *before* you crash - not after

Task Transitions

Transitions can be especially challenging for ADHD brains, which often struggle with task inertia - the difficulty of stopping one activity and starting another. Without support, shifting gears can feel overwhelming or even paralysing. That's why building in transition rituals is so helpful. Simple actions like making a cup of tea, stretching, or changing your environment signal to your brain that it's time to switch focus. Countdown timers help prepare mentally, while buffer time between events reduces pressure and allows you to reset. These gentle pauses create space for smoother transitions and help reduce stress, making your day feel more manageable and intentional.

- Create "transition rituals" between activities (e.g., a cup of tea before moving from work to home tasks).
- Use countdown timers to prepare for shifting tasks.
- Give yourself *buffer time* between events.

Emotional Regulation

Emotional regulation can be one of the most challenging aspects of ADHD, especially when big feelings come on fast and strong. Rather than suppressing or judging these emotions, it's helpful to create a calm-down toolkit - practical, sensory strategies that bring your nervous system back into balance. Whether it's the weight of a blanket, a grounding scent, or a few deep breaths, these tools remind your body it's safe. Pair them with affirmations and grounding exercises to reconnect with the present moment. Most importantly, give yourself permission to feel. Emotions are not weaknesses - they are signals. Acknowledging them without shame is a powerful act of self-acceptance and healing.

- Keep a calm-down toolkit: weighted blanket, calming scents, breathing exercises.
- Use affirmations or grounding techniques ("Name 5 things you can see…").
- Acknowledge big feelings without shame - they're valid.

Communicating Needs

For many neurodivergent people, expressing needs can feel vulnerable, especially when past experiences include being misunderstood or dismissed. Using scripts or pre-written messages can ease that pressure and help you advocate for yourself clearly and calmly. Communicating preferences - like needing time to reply or space to process - builds trust and prevents miscommunication. And just as importantly, learning to say "no" with kindness is a vital skill, not just in protecting your time, but in honouring your energy and boundaries. Clear, compassionate communication is not a weakness—it's a strength that creates deeper, more authentic connections with others and with yourself.

- Use scripts or pre-written messages if communication feels hard.
- Let people know your preferences: "I may not reply straight away, but I care."
- Practice saying "no" gently and with kindness (to yourself too).

Spirituality & Intention Setting

Manifesting With ADHD + Building a Life With Purpose

Spirituality has always been a quiet but powerful thread in my life - not loud or traditional, but deeply personal. As someone with ADHD, my mind is always moving, always dreaming, always envisioning. For a long time, I saw that as a flaw. Now, I see it as a gift.

People with ADHD are natural visionaries. We live in possibilities, not limitations. That's why manifesting - visualising something and working towards it - can be so powerful for us. When paired with intention and grounded action, it's like planting a seed and watching it bloom.

Manifesting With ADHD: A Gentle Guide
1.   **Picture It Clearly**

Close your eyes and imagine the thing you want. Not just what it looks like - but how it *feels*. Where are you? What are you wearing? What do you smell, touch, hear? The more detailed, the better.

2.   **Put It Somewhere You'll See It**

Make a vision board or write it down in your journal. Use voice notes if writing's not your thing. Keep that goal *visible* - it helps with object permanence.

3. **Act as If**

Ask yourself: "What would the version of me who already has this be doing today?" Show up for that version. You don't have to be perfect - just consistent in your intention.

4. **Take Aligned Action**

Manifesting isn't just dreaming - it's planting seeds *and* watering them. Take small, actionable steps toward your goal. Trust the process, even when it's slow.

5. **Let Go of Perfection**

ADHD brains are often all-or-nothing. Remind yourself: messy action is better than no action. You don't have to get it right the first time.

The Gratitude Ritual: 3 Small Things

Gratitude grounds us - especially when our minds feel scattered.

Every morning, write down or say aloud 3 things you're grateful for. They don't have to be big:
- "The way my coffee smells this morning"
- "A message from a friend yesterday"
- "Getting the kids ready without stress"

The goal isn't perfection. It's presence. When we practise gratitude, we rewire our brains to look for good - and suddenly, good finds us more often.

7. Letting Go & Moving Forward

There comes a point on the healing journey when we must pause - not to chase something new, but to release what no longer belongs to us.

Healing isn't just about learning new things. It's about unlearning what was never true to begin with. It's about **letting go of the shame, the stories, and the survival**

masks, and making space for something more aligned - **more you.**

We don't owe the world a polished version of ourselves. We owe ourselves the truth.

What I'm Leaving Behind
- The shame of not fitting in
- The belief that I am "too much" or "not enough"
- The stories I was told - or told myself - about who I had to be
- The mask I wore to survive
- The guilt for needing rest
- The people-pleasing and boundary-blurring that came from fear
- The idea that I have to do everything alone

These were never mine to carry. They were survival tools, not my truth.

What I'm Growing Into

- A deep trust in my own intuition
- Confidence rooted in who I am - not who I think I should be
- A life lived in alignment, not performance
- Rest without guilt
- Friendships that honour the real me
- Creativity, passion, purpose
- A new story - one I choose for myself

Your Turn: What Are You Leaving Behind?

What are you ready to release? Shame? People-pleasing? A story that no longer serves you?

Take a moment. Breathe. When you're ready, finish the sentences:

- **I'm letting go of…**

- **I'm growing into…**

- **The version of me I'm becoming feels…**

Letting go is not a one-time act. It's a practice. And every time you choose your truth over your mask, you're already moving forward

Neurodivergent Joy Journal Prompts

Use these prompts when you feel lost in the noise. They help reconnect you to joy and authenticity.

- • What lit me up today?

- • When did I feel most like me?

- • What did I do that felt nourishing, not just productive?

- • What made me laugh recently?

- • What felt easy today?

Creative Regulation Tools

Not all grounding techniques work for everyone. Here are a few creative or sensory-based tools to help regulate during overwhelm:

- • Doodling with your non-dominant hand
- • Ripping paper slowly and mindfully
- • Using sensory putty or playdough
- • Tracing mandalas or colouring with music
- • Creating a calming 'sensory shelf' with textures, scents, and visuals

What I Wish I Knew Sooner

A list of truths learned the hard way. Feel free to add your own.

- • I'm not lazy, I'm overstimulated.
- • Saying no isn't mean - it's kind to myself.
- • I can mother in my own way - and that's enough.
- • My intuition isn't a weakness, it's a compass.
- • Rest is productive too.

❀ Helpful Tips for an ADHD Mother

Because neurodivergent motherhood deserves understanding, grace, and practical support

1. Embrace Imperfect Parenting

You do not need to be a perfect parent - you just need to be a *present* one. There will be days where things feel chaotic. You may forget the PE kit, burn the dinner, or feel like you've lost your patience. That's okay. Repair matters more than perfection. Apologise when needed, model healthy emotional expression, and remind yourself - being human is enough.

2. Create ADHD-Friendly Systems

Structure helps ADHD brains thrive. But your systems don't have to look like anyone else's. Try:

- A whiteboard for school events and reminders
- Daily checklists for both you and your children
- Using Alexa or phone alarms to manage routines
- Batching tasks like washing uniforms on one set day
- Colour-coding or simplifying wherever possible (e.g. same sock colours!)

3. The "Good Enough" Rule

Don't fall into the trap of thinking things need to be done *perfectly* to count. A partially tidied room is still better than a messy one. A sandwich for dinner is still a meal. Your kids won't remember if your floors were clean - they'll remember if they felt loved.

4. Prioritise Self-Regulation

You can't pour from an empty cup. When you're overstimulated or overwhelmed, take mini breaks:

- Deep breathing in the bathroom

- Putting on noise-cancelling headphones
- Saying "Mum needs a moment, I'll be right back"

It's not selfish. It's essential.

5. Externalise the Chaos

ADHD brains hold too much inside. Try:

- Brain-dumping thoughts and tasks into a notebook or app
- Sticky notes for key reminders
- Putting visual cues *where you need to see them* (e.g., lunchboxes on the door handle)

6. Ask for Help Without Shame

Being a parent with ADHD is a heavy load. You're not failing by needing help -you're being resourceful. Whether it's school staff, friends, or professionals, let people know what would make a difference for you. You don't have to carry everything alone.

7. Use Hyperfocus When It Helps - But Watch for Burnout

There will be days where you feel like a super mum - hyper focused and achieving all the things. Let yourself ride that wave. Just don't forget to eat, drink, or rest. Balance intensity with recovery.

8. Reframe the Guilt

That guilt you feel? It comes from caring *so much*. But it's okay to let go of shame. ADHD parenting might look different - but different doesn't mean wrong. It often means creative, compassionate, and deeply attuned.

9. Connect With Others Who Get It

You are not alone. Whether through online communities, books like this, or friends you meet on the journey - connection is key. Find your people and remind each other: you're doing great.

10. Leave Space for Joy

Amongst the to-do lists and meltdowns, there is joy. Tiny hands reaching for yours. The way they call "Mum!" a hundred times a day because *you* are their safe place. The cuddles at bedtime. Let yourself soak in those moments - they are your fuel, your why, your everything.

Reflection pages

These pages are your space.

To pause. To breathe. To untangle the thoughts that swirl in your neurodivergent mind.

Reflection is not about getting it "right." It's about permitting yourself to *feel*, to *process*, and to *be*. Here, you can let your thoughts roam freely - no judgement, no pressure.

You might write a sentence, a poem, a memory, or a list. You might just doodle or stare at the page until the words come. Whatever you do, let it be yours.

There's wisdom inside you. These pages are here to help you hear it.

Final Note: A Message Beyond the Mask

If you've made it to this page, thank you. Thank you for walking alongside me, through the chaos and clarity, the shadows and the light. This book is not just my story, it's a hand to hold, a reminder that you are never alone in your mess or your magic. You are not too much. You are not too late. You are not broken.

The world may have tried to silence your voice, question your worth, or label you in ways that never truly fit. But beyond every mask you've worn, whether to survive, to belong, or to protect yourself, there has always been *you*. Whole. Worthy. Wildly enough. This is not the end. This is a beginning. Of reclaiming your narrative. Of writing your next chapter with courage, compassion, and truth. So go forward - unmasked, unfiltered, unapologetically you. Because your story matters. And you were never meant to hide. With love and solidarity,

Kayleigh

Author's Note

These pages hold my truth, not the kind carved in stone,
But the kind etched in feeling, in memory, in the soft ache of lived experience.

I write not to accuse, but to express.
Not to expose, but to heal.

No names are contained.
Some moments may blur between what was said and what was felt.
But all of it is real to me.

This is my story, through my eyes,
where memory and emotion often dance more vividly than fact ever could.

List of Helpful resources

Domestic Violence & Emotional Abuse

- **Refuge – National Domestic Abuse Helpline**
  0808 2000 247 (24/7, free, confidential)
  www.nationaldahelpline.org.uk
  For women and children experiencing domestic violence. Includes live chat, support planning, and resources.
- **Women's Aid**
  www.womensaid.org.uk
  Support for women experiencing abuse, including an online chat and directory of local services.
- **SurvivorsUK**
  www.survivorsuk.org
  Specialist support for men, boys, and non-binary people who've experienced sexual abuse or assault.

Miscarriage, Baby Loss & Grief

- **The Miscarriage Association**
  01924 200799
  www.miscarriageassociation.org.uk
  Offers information, support groups, and helplines

for those affected by miscarriage and pregnancy loss.

- **Sands – Stillbirth and Neonatal Death Charity**
  0808 164 3332

  www.sands.org.uk

  Bereavement support for those who have lost a baby.

Depression, Trauma & Suicidal Thoughts

- **Samaritans**
  116 123 (24/7, free)

  www.samaritans.org

  Confidential support for anyone in emotional distress, crisis, or suicidal thoughts.

- **Mind**

  www.mind.org.uk

  Offers mental health information and local support options.

- **Shout 85258**

  Text **SHOUT** to 85258 (24/7)

  www.giveusashout.org

  Free, confidential text service for anyone in crisis.

- **Rethink Mental Illness**

  www.rethink.org

Practical advice and support for living with mental illness.

For Trauma Survivors

- **The National Association for People Abused in Childhood (NAPAC)**
  0808 801 0331
  www.napac.org.uk
  For adults who have experienced childhood abuse, offering support and recovery resources.
- **The Survivors Trust**
  www.thesurvivorstrust.org
  Directory of local rape and sexual abuse support services across the UK.
- **Trauma Research UK**
  www.traumaresearchuk.org
  Self-help programmes and support for those living with PTSD, trauma, and phobias.

Other Useful Services

- **Hub of Hope**
  www.hubofhope.co.uk

A national database of mental health support—enter your postcode to find local help.

- **NHS IAPT (Improving Access to Psychological Therapies)**
  www.nhs.uk/mental-health
  You can self-refer for free NHS counselling and therapy services in most areas.

You are not broken. You are healing.

Please don't suffer in silence - reach out and take small steps forward. Healing isn't linear, but you don't have to walk it alone.

References

Attention Deficit Disorder Association. (2023). Understanding Hyperfocus. https://add.org/hyperfocus/

ADHD Foundation. (2021). Girls and ADHD: Underdiagnosed and Misunderstood. https://www.adhdfoundation.org.uk

Armstrong, T. (2010). *Neurodiversity: Discovering the Extraordinary Gifts of Autism, ADHD, Dyslexia, and Other Brain Differences.* Da Capo Press.

Barkley, R. A. (2015). Attention-Deficit Hyperactivity Disorder: A Handbook for Diagnosis and Treatment (4th ed.). Guilford Press.

Chronis-Tuscano, A., Seymour, K. E., Stein, M. A., Jones, H. A., & Jiles, C. D. (2008). The role of parental ADHD in the development of child ADHD and associated outcomes: A review of the empirical literature. Journal of Child and Family Studies, 17(5), 563–584. https://doi.org/10.1007/s10826-007-9175-2

Baron-Cohen, S., & Wheelwright, S. (2004). *The empathy quotient: An investigation of adults with Asperger syndrome or high functioning autism, and normal sex differences.* Journal of Autism and Developmental Disorders, 34(2), 163–175. https://doi.org/10.1023/B:JADD.0000022607.19833.00

Barkley, R. A. (2015). *Attention-deficit hyperactivity disorder: A handbook for diagnosis and treatment.* Guilford Publications.

Bird, G., Silani, G., Brindley, R., White, S., Frith, U., & Singer, T. (2010). *Empathic brain responses in insula are modulated by levels of alexithymia but not autism.* Brain, 133(5), 1515–1525. https://doi.org/10.1093/brain/awq060

Buckner, R. L., Andrews-Hanna, J. R., & Schacter, D. L. (2008). *The brain's default network: anatomy, function, and relevance to disease.* Annals of the New York Academy of Sciences, 1124(1), 1–38.

Carnes, P. (2017). *The Betrayal Bond: Breaking Free of Exploitive Relationships* (2nd ed.). Health Communications, Inc.

Done ADHD. (2023). *ADHD and empathy: A deep dive.* Retrieved from https://www.donefirst.com/blog/adhd-and-empathy

Dodson, W. (2020). Emotional Dysregulation and Rejection Sensitivity in ADHD. ADDitude Magazine. https://www.additudemag.com/emotional-dysregulation-adhd-rsd/

Embrace Autism. (2022). Autistic Impostor Syndrome. https://embrace-autism.com/autistic-impostor-syndrome/

Doyle, G. (2020). Untamed. Dial Press.

Groen, Y., den Heijer, A. E., Fuermaier, A. B. M., Althaus, M., & Tucha, O. (2018). The role of empathy and emotion recognition in social functioning in individuals with ADHD. *Journal of Attention Disorders, 22*(9), 838–853. https://doi.org/10.1177/1087054715575064

Gill, T. (2014). *The Benefits of Children's Engagement with Nature: A Systematic Literature Review.* Children, Youth and Environments, 24(2), 10–34.

Hallowell, E. (2021). *ADHD and empathy.* The Hallowell Todaro ADHD Center. Retrieved from https://www.hallowelltodaro.com/blog-raw-feed/2021/1/28/adhd-and-empathy

Hartman, C. A., et al. (2022). Moral sensitivity and empathy in adults with ADHD. Journal of Neurodevelopmental Disorders, 14(1), 12.

Inclusive Teach. (2024). Managing ADHD and Codependency: Strategies for Improved Quality of Life. Retrieved from https://inclusiveteach.com

Kellert, S. R. (2005). *Building for life: Designing and understanding the human-nature connection.* Island Press.

McCurdy, L. E., Winterbottom, K. E., Mehta, S. S., & Roberts, J. R. (2010). Using nature and outdoor activity to improve children's health. *Current Problems in Pediatric and Adolescent Health Care, 40*(5), 102–117.

Milton, D. (2012). *On the ontological status of autism: the 'double empathy problem'.* Disability & Society, 27(6), 883–887. https://doi.org/10.1080/09687599.2012.710008

Riviera Therapy. (2024). ADHD and Codependency in Relationships. Retrieved from https://rivieratherapy.com

Ramsay, J. R., & Rostain, A. L. (2021). The impact of late diagnosis of ADHD in women: A qualitative study. Journal of Attention Disorders, 25(6), 741-750.

SimplyWellbeing. (2022). *ADHD intuition: Seeing beyond the obvious.* Retrieved from https://www.simplywellbeing.com/insights/being-adhd/adhd-intuition/

Self. (2024). Dating with ADHD: How to Build Healthier Relationships. Retrieved from https://www.self.com/story/dating-relationships-adhd

Singer, J. (1999). *'Why can't you be normal for once in your life?' From a 'problem with no name' to the emergence of a new category of difference.* In M. Corker & S. French (Eds.), Disability Discourse. Open University Press.

Shiffrin, R. M., & Schneider, W. (1977). *Controlled and automatic human information processing: II. Perceptual learning, automatic attending and a general theory.* Psychological Review, 84(2), 127–190.

Tivers, E. (2020). The ADHD Brain and Imposter Syndrome. ADHD ReWired Podcast.

The Wave Clinic. (2023). *ADHD superpowers: Hyperfocus, creativity and intuition.* Retrieved from https://thewaveclinic.com/blog/adhd-superpowers-hyperfocus-creativity-intuition

Verywell Mind. (2024). ADHD and Toxic Relationships. Retrieved from https://www.verywellmind.com/adhd-and-toxic-relationships-6831288

Wikipedia. (2025). Attention-Deficit Hyperactivity Disorder (ADHD). Retrieved from https://en.wikipedia.org/wiki/Attention-deficit_hyperactivity_disorder_(ADHD)

Walker, N. (2021). *Neuroqueer Heresies: Notes on the Neurodiversity Paradigm, Autistic Empowerment, and Postnormal Possibilities.* Autonomous Press.

White, H. A., & Shah, P. (2006). Uninhibited imaginations: Creativity in adults with Attention-Deficit/Hyperactivity Disorder. Personality and Individual Differences, 40(6), 1121–1131.

Young, S., Adamo, N., Ásgeirsdóttir, B. B., Branney, P., Beckett, M., Colley, W., & Gudjonsson, G. (2022). Females with ADHD: An expert consensus statement taking a lifespan approach providing guidance for the identification and treatment of attention-deficit/hyperactivity disorder in girls and women. BMC Psychiatry, 22, 284.

Zhang, S., Lin, B., & Feng, Y. (2020). Hyperfocus in Adults with ADHD: A Neuropsychological Perspective. Neuropsychology Review, 30(3), 456–470.

Printed in Dunstable, United Kingdom

67237442R00143